How We "Do" School

Poems to Encourage Teacher Reflection

Karen Morrow Durica

INTERNATIONAL
Reading Association
800 BARKSDALE ROAD, PO BOX 8139
NEWARK, DE 19714-8139, USA
www.reading.org

D1275832

The International Reading Association attempts, through its publications, to provide a forum for a wide spectrum of opinions on reading. This policy permits divergent viewpoints without implying the endorsement of the Association.

Executive Editor, Books   Corinne M. Mooney
Developmental Editor   Charlene M. Nichols
Developmental Editor   Tori Mello Bachman
Developmental Editor   Stacey Lynn Sharp
Editorial Production Manager   Shannon T. Fortner
Production Manager   Iona Muscella
Supervisor, Electronic Publishing   Anette Schuetz
Project Editor   Charlene M. Nichols
Production Editor   Christina Lambert

Cover   Design, Linda Steere; Photograph, © Getty Images; Inset photos (from top left), © Jupiter Images Corporation, © Comstock Images, © Comstock Images, © Comstock Images.

Library of Congress Cataloging-in-Publication Data

Durica, Karen Morrow.
  How we "do" school : poems to encourage teacher reflection / Karen Morrow Durica.
    p. cm.
  Includes bibliographical references and index.
  ISBN-13: 978-0-87207-610-5
  1. Teaching--Poetry. 2. Teachers--Poetry. I. Title.
  PS3604.U75H69 2007
  811'.6--dc22
                                                                2006034515

In loving memory of my mother
—Josephine Skrovan Morrow—
for always loving a little girl's poems

Contents

Section IV

REFLECTIONS ABOUT THE IMPACT OF TEACHERS AND PARENTS

Section V

REFLECTIONS ABOUT THE REWARDS OF TEACHING

About the Author

Karen Morrow Durica received a Bachelor of Science in Education from St. John College of Cleveland, Ohio, USA (now part of Ursuline College, Pepper Pike, Ohio), and a Master of Arts in Reading from the University of Colorado at Denver, USA. Her professional experience includes the following: elementary classroom teacher, literacy specialist, K–12 language arts coordinator, district staff developer, early intervention trainer, district literacy coordinator, K–12 Director of Curriculum and Instruction, and adjunct instructor at several universities in Colorado. She has served as a literacy consultant in various states and is a frequent presenter at the annual conference of the Colorado Council International Reading Association (CCIRA). In addition, Karen is a member of the Colorado Governor's Advisory Board for the statewide Read to Achieve program and served two years as editor of CCIRA's newsletter *Colorado Communicator*.

Karen's published works include *Literature Links to Phonics: A Balanced Approach* (1996) and the chapter "An Early Reading Intervention Program for Children Who Struggle" in *What It Takes to Be a Teacher: The Role of Personal and Professional Development* (Freppon, 2001). Karen also has published poetry and numerous articles in state literacy journals.

Recently retired after 35 years in education, Karen remains passionate about literacy, serving on several CCIRA committees. *Ancora imparo* (I am still learning—attributed to Italian Renaissance sculptor, painter, architect, and poet Michelangelo in 1552 when he was 87 years old) remains her mantra, as she presently is studying Spanish and piano. Karen enjoys reading, writing, yoga, and walking in the Colorado sunshine. She and her husband, Ed, have three grown children. Her favorite pastime is reading aloud to her grandchildren.

Author Information for Correspondence and Workshops

Please feel free to contact the author with comments and questions about this book. Karen's e-mail address is duricadive@comcast.net.

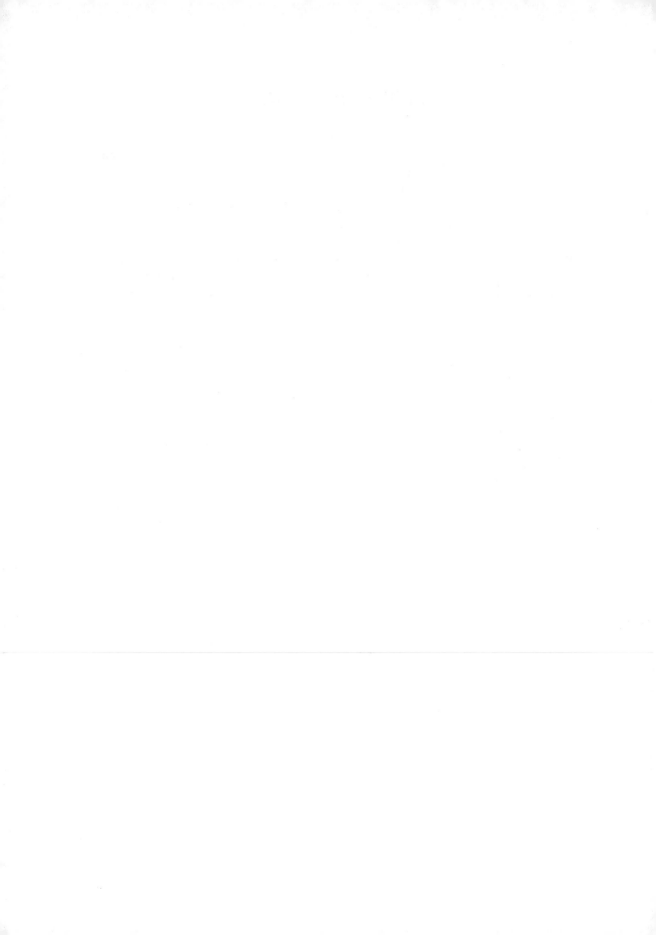

Preface

"Let us put our minds together and see what life we can make for our children."

SITTING BULL, TATANKA-IYOTANKA (1831–1890)

This is a book of reflections—my reflections over 35 years as an educator, based on actual events or comments from my students. Nearly a century ago, philosopher, psychologist, and education reformer John Dewey, who wrote about reflection as a "specialized form of thinking" (as cited in Stewart, Prebble, & Duncan, 1997, p. 161), reminded us that we do not learn from our experiences; we learn from *thinking* about our experiences. Throughout my career as a classroom teacher, literacy specialist, and staff developer, I kept a journal. I recorded moments of delight and triumph as well as moments of rage, frustration, or disappointment over my own actions or those of colleagues. Often, my journal note was just a phrase or two; at other times, my emotions were so powerful they compelled me to write a poem—my catharsis since early childhood. Periodically rereading those notes and poems—and reflecting on their messages—contributed to my growth and refinement as a teacher. My reflections were catalysts for some of the more significant changes I made in my philosophical and instructional stance toward teaching: My reflections changed the way I interacted with students, changed the way I presented difficult lessons, and greatly added to the privilege and honor I felt in being able to spend my professional life before such amazing children. I was inspired to put my mind to making a better life—because what makes their school experiences better tends to make their lives better—for my students.

The impetus for these reflections was the children themselves; they were my constant and valued teachers. Each poem in this collection is based on an experience with or a comment from an actual student. To this day, I can see the faces of those cherished young people who continually taught me what school needed to be like in order for all children to be successful. The poems do not cover every major area of current educational concern because I wanted to remain true to the integrity and the heart of this book: the journey from actual incident, to journal note, to poem, to reflection. Therefore, if I had not entered a journal note about an event that addressed a particular issue, I did not include a poem about that issue in this collection. However, the poems that are included do address important and common issues, such as educational environment and organization, curriculum, diversity, teacher and parental impact, and the passion and joy of our work. Some poems spring from incidents at specific grade levels or in specific content areas, but the messages they carry cross those parameters because the messages focus on students: how they learn, why they learn, and who they are as learners. Although my teaching career was far more joyful and rewarding than not, the majority of the poems highlight areas begging for reform. Those areas spurred me to deepest reflection and subsequent change. It is my hope that these poems present for you a beginning for reflective practice.

This set of poems and reflections takes its title from the first poem, "How We Do School," which epitomizes the underlying theme of the entire collection. Just as we "do" laundry in a certain way—we gather, sort, wash, and dry—so, too, we "do" school. As educators, we gather students, we sort them (by grade level, ability, or both), we teach them, we test them, and we grade them. We either pass them along or return them for an additional cycle. The regimen that is school is quite similar across the United States, and long-standing organizational as well as pedagogical practices are seldom questioned. They are accepted because "that's how it's done in school." Simply, *that's how we do school.* As I strongly suggest through these poems, it would behoove educators to take a thoughtful look at some of those practices if we seriously want *all* students to be successful.

Following this preface is a section with tips for effectively using reflective poetry as part of staff development. The organization of the remainder of the book provides educators with the poem first, as the impact of the poems—without explanation—is what most inspires dynamic discussion. Following each poem is background information and connection to current educational practice. Reflective questions and suggested action, based on the design promoted in Lipton and Wellman's (2003) work on reflective practice, follow. I have found this design to be particularly effective because it not only invites teachers to participate in reflective conversations but also calls for action, investigation, and application. Within this structure, teachers are able to more readily move from discussion to concrete changes. Each section concludes with a list of several resources for more in-depth reading on the topic. The poems have been grouped into five categories: (1) school environment, (2) curriculum, (3) diversity, (4) teacher and parental impact, and (5) rewards of teaching. Although these groupings include poems with similar themes, they are not intended to restrict a poem's use, as poetry often sparks diverse thinking and calls forth unanticipated reactions based on individual memories. In addition, several of the poems incorporate multiple themes, and liberal implementation is encouraged. Refer to the following section on using reflective poetry for additional considerations.

I have used these poems as part of preservice- and graduate-level education courses and have experienced the reward of teachers engaging in profound and provocative discussions. Weeks later, teachers return and announce they have changed something in their classroom routine or incorporated a different approach with a student "because of that poem we talked about in class." Lyons and Pinnell (2001) list creating "a culture that encourages reflection" (p. 46) as one of the 10 most important actions leading to effective professional development. This core collection of poems and suggested reflections can lay a foundation for such a culture. Once it becomes common practice to reflect on events, behaviors, and actions, many situations can promote reflection. In their work *Reflective Practice to Improve Schools*, York-Barr, Sommers, Ghere, and Montie (2001) state,

> Reflection on experience is the pathway to improvement. Reflection is a means for examining beliefs, assumptions and practices. It can lead to increased insights about instructional effectiveness. It can also result in the discovery of incongruities between espoused beliefs and actual actions. (p. xvii)

It is my hope that these poems—these lessons from my students—will present opportunities for reflection and will contribute to building a reflective approach to educational practice, thus enabling teachers to refine their work. As you read these poems, you will not be able to see the cherished faces of the children, but know...they are there. Revisiting them as I put together this collection truly made this work a labor of love.

Acknowledgments

I thank each and every student who has ever blessed my life. I have learned so much from each of you, and my life is richer because you have been a part of it. I also thank my friend and colleague Dr. Michael Opitz for encouraging me to share my work with a larger audience.

Additional Resources for Engaging in Reflective Practice

Bambino, D. (2002). Critical friends. *Educational Leadership, 59*(6), 25–27.

Eisner, E. (2003). Questionable assumptions about schooling. *Phi Delta Kappan, 84*(9), 648–657.

Kuzmeskus, J. (Ed). (1996). *We teach them all: Teachers writing about diversity.* Portland, ME: Stenhouse.

Layne, S.L. (2001). *Life's literacy lessons: Poems for teachers.* Newark, DE: International Reading Association.

Sparks, D. (1998). The educator, examined. *Journal of Staff Development, 19*(3), 38–42.

Tips for Using Reflective Poetry as Part of Professional Development

"Reflection is the beginning of reform."

MARK TWAIN (1835–1910)

The role of staff development is vital to the pursuit of excellence we, as educators, expect in all our schools. Darling-Hammond emphasizes that well-informed teachers have a greater impact on student achievement than specific programs: "My research and personal experience tell me that the single most important determinant of success for a student is the knowledge and skills of that child's teacher" (as cited in Goldberg, 2001, p. 689). It is not uncommon for school districts to spend thousands of dollars on programs and materials without seeing the desired results in student achievement because the teachers implementing those new programs and using those new materials have not grown in their understanding about the underlying theory of learning and classroom pedagogy. Staff development that incorporates reflection allows teachers to go beyond being receptacles of information and encourages them to thoughtfully implement changes that can make a difference to their students. Routman (2002) suggests, "Even the best professional development may fail to create meaningful and lasting changes in teaching and learning—unless teachers engage in ongoing professional dialogue to develop a reflective school community" (p. 32).

The poems in this collection are meant to promote reflective conversation. They are not intended to be "interpreted" or analyzed line by line. They are stories—true stories about how children feel and respond to how we, as educators, do school. Each poem, on its own merit, will say something to the teachers who read it, but that message may differ depending on the knowledge and past experiences of the reader. That not only is OK—it's desirable!

By resurrecting beliefs and feelings about school, teachers can begin to reflect on their own practices. Through that reflection, reform becomes a possibility. If you previously have not used reflection as part of your staff development, you may be surprised to find that it does not come easily to some teachers. In *What It Takes to Be a Teacher: The Role of Personal and Professional Development*, Freppon (2001) states, "Reflection involves conflicting thoughts and questions. It is hard work and it can be painful. Acting professionally on reflection requires true grit" (p. 2). So rule number one: Be gentle and be patient.

Following are some specific ideas about how to use these poems and the reflective questions and extended activities. They are suggestions based on what I have found to be successful, but they by no means are mandates. Feel free to use your own sense of where and how reflective poetry may fit into your work.

1. Choose one poem; there is no need to discuss them in a given order. If you are just beginning reflective practice, select a poem with a theme that may be especially meaningful to the teachers.

2. Read aloud the poem. The impact of the poem, without explanation, background or additional information, is most essential to prompting discussion.

3. Avoid lengthy analysis of the poem. Allow teachers to simply state what the poem says to them. And remember, there are no right and wrong answers.

4. Allow adequate time for conversation. Don't rush into the reflective questions or the extended activity. Depending on the given time frame, the reflective questions or activity may be postponed for a following session.

5. Share the background information provided after the initial discussion. Understanding that the poem is rooted in actual student comments or events is an important element of this particular collection of poems.

6. Allow teachers to select which reflective question they would like to pursue, when possible. Just as the poem itself may carry a different message for individual teachers, so, too, the usefulness of the reflective questions will weigh differently for them. When teachers have a choice, the time spent in serious, reflective thought will be more meaningful to them. Keep in mind that teacher time is at a premium. Avoid making reflection an "assignment" that becomes a burden rather than an invigorating intellectual and professional pursuit.

7. Provide time for teachers to share their insights or questions after reflection. A hallmark of genuine reflection is that it often gives rise to more questions than it does answers. Don't ignore the questions that are raised. Chart them somewhere, and periodically revisit them to discuss the status of the situation that was the basis for the question.

8. Ensure that teachers have adequate time and support to participate in the extended activity. Ideally, participation should be on a voluntary basis. Again, the activity should not be "one more thing" the teachers are asked to do. Approach the activity with a "teacher–researcher" frame of mind; that is, make sure that teachers have the opportunity to share their findings and receive appropriate recognition for taking extra steps to refine their practice.

9. Spend the time you need with each poem, but watch for signs of exhausting the topic. Let the teachers be your guide. Even if you feel a particular issue has not been explored to the depth you would have preferred, it is better to revisit that issue a few months later than try to wring every ounce of worth from the poem and questions once you sense that the teachers' store of conversation about the issue has been drained.

10. While working with a poem, post it in the office or teachers' lounge and ensure that each teacher has his or her own copy. This will enable teachers to keep the issue upfront and present and will help thinkers who need to allow the topic to incubate before they form ideas and opinions.

11. Ask teachers to find additional poems or excerpts from literature, professional reading, or student work (respecting student ownership) that can be used to spark reflective thinking about educational practice.

12. Make reflection a part of your common practice. Establish a routine where certain meetings or gatherings begin (or end) with reflection. Periodically, evaluate the reflective process with the teachers and determine whether they are finding the approach enjoyable and helpful in refining their work.

Section I

REFLECTIONS ABOUT

SCHOOL ENVIRONMENT

"If an educational system has only universal goals and a limited variety of educational approaches, it is not surprising that the results for many students will end in failure. This is because these students did not fit the system. It is not entirely the students who are fixed and unchangeable; it is also the system."

JACQUELINE GRENNON BROOKS & MARTIN G. BROOKS (1993, p. 60)

How We Do School

*A*sk yourself:

Is it truly easier for *all* to sit and learn?
Should 8-year-olds *all* share the same ability and concern?

Does *everyone* learn better when there's silence in the room?
Do 50-minute periods give *all* the time to bloom?

Is the *only* way to learn about geometry from a book?
Are having five neat paragraphs how *each* essay should look?

Does *every* brain work at its best at 7:45?
Do practice tests for seven weeks make *everybody* thrive?

Does *every* learner need a break at exactly the same time?
Are projects better if each one must have the *same* design?

Does only *certain* literature make somebody a reader?
Do *only* sports, or math, or speech make somebody a leader?

Can *everyone* show what is known by way of written tests?
Does giving "points" inspire *all* to do their very best?

Does compliance to the rules of school define a *better* student?
Is it *possible* the misfits are as able, bright, and prudent?

Appears if we look closely at the structures we embrace—
Creating hardships for some students, making school a hampered place;

We'd understand that many problems seem to be *our* fault—
How we do school is often for convenience of *adults*.

Background: How We Do School

Early in my career as an educator, I was impressed with the seminal work of Marie Clay (1979), particularly her emphasis on observing children. Without a doubt, the most useful skill I developed in my career was the skill of "kid watching" (Goodman, 1985). As I became more adept at observing how children learn, I realized two things: (1) Through careful observation, children will show you how they best learn, and (2) many of the established practices and historical structures of how we do school actually inhibit the progress some learners could make. Often, these practices and structures force students to forsake approaches to learning that are most effective for them. As Goodlad states in *A Place Called School: Prospects for the Future* (1984), "Nowhere else [but in schools] are large groups of individuals packed so closely together for so many hours, yet expected to perform at peak efficiency on difficult learning tasks and to interact harmoniously" (p. 86).

The realization that how we do school may be part of the problem for many students became evident the year I was working as a literacy specialist, supporting a first grader who was struggling with reading. When we worked together, I allowed her to stand and lean against the table while she read. She would alternate among swaying from foot to foot, wiggling her bottom, and standing up straight. She had told me that that's how she liked to read. However, this behavior was not permitted in her classroom. Her teacher informed me that if she let one student do it, all would want to do it and "that's just not how we read in school." That classroom standard did not change even after I demonstrated how much longer the student read for me, and how much more proficiently she performed.

I began to think of other school practices that possibly interfere with students' learning needs. "How We Do School" evolved from observing many readily accepted practices and questioning whether the students or the adults benefited most from them.

Reflection Questions

1. What school structures made learning easy for you? Which made learning more difficult? Why? Discuss your response with a colleague. How are your responses similar? Where do you differ? What implications might your responses have for what you do in your classroom?

   _____

   _____

   _____

   _____

   _____

   _____

2. Teachers also have preferences, styles, and needs. How can you balance your needs as an individual with the needs of your students? During the next month or two, determine if there is an area of student interest or need that is particularly difficult for you to accommodate. Brainstorm with a colleague about possible plans of action.

   _____

   _____

   _____

   _____

   _____

   _____

3. Visualize the perfect school. What would be included in that school that is missing from the one in which you presently teach? What might be eliminated? Share your vision with a colleague. Is there one element of your present situation that you can change to move toward that more perfect idea?

   _____

   _____

   _____

   _____

   _____

   _____

Extended Activity

Select one of the following researchers and the corresponding topic: Brian Cambourne (conditions of learning), Howard Gardner (multiple intelligences), or Carol Ann Tomlinson (differentiation). Investigate what the selected educator recommends about creating environments to meet students' diverse needs. What recommendations do you already have in place? What could be a goal for the future refinement of your practice?

_____

_____

_____

_____

_____

_____

_____

_____

_____

_____

_____

_____

_____

_____

_____

_____

_____

_____

_____

_____

_____

_____

_____

_____

_____

_____

_____

I Used to Ask the Questions: Kindergartner's Lament

I used to ask the questions.
    I used to play for hours
        and learn so many things.
    I used to watch how something happened
      and then try it by myself
      till my own effort found its wings.

I used to pick the books we'd read at naptime.
    I used to know the stories
      all by heart.
    I used to listen to the sounds those friendly words made
      and play with silly rhymes
      and change the parts.

I used to write great stories for my teddy.
    I used words that made
      my daddy smile or sigh.
    I used to make the letters in green crayon
      And if I wanted—just for fun—
      I'd decorate the *i*'s.

I used to feel my world was so exciting!
    I used to wonder about things
      from stars to sand.
    I used to think my questions weren't a bother
      and my answers—right or wrong—
      were always grand.

I remember that I used to ask the questions.
    I remember
      just how learning made me feel.
    I remember how I loved to think
      and puzzle
      and how the word *discovery* was real.

Yes, I remember that I used to ask the questions...
    and then...
    I started school.

Background:
I Used to Ask the Questions: Kindergartner's Lament

I taught kindergarten for one year of my career. It was an extraordinary year—an experience I wish every teacher, whether elementary, secondary, or postsecondary, could have at least once in his or her journey as an educator. You see miracles every day. My own three children were born by that time, and (as any parent will attest) I knew, of course, that all three of them were brilliant! What I realized as a kindergarten teacher was that *everyone's* children were brilliant. I am not saying that in some "warm and fuzzy," "oh, they're all so sweet" way; I make this statement with the seriousness of a professional observer of learners. I had 25 students in the morning and 25 in the afternoon. From the first day of school, each of those 50 children awed me with his or her knowledge. I kept musing, "These little ones have been on this earth only 60 months, and look what they already know; look what they already can do." The more I reflected on this astounding situation, the more I thought about how they learned it all. For the most part, they had controlled a majority of their own learning—*they had asked the questions*.

When students ask questions because they genuinely want to know the answer, they are intrinsically motivated to listen to and to remember the response. Current researchers confirm the importance of motivation and the impact of students recognizing the purpose of what they are learning, and sensing that they have some control over it (Cambourne, 1995; Schlechty, 2002; Smith & Wilhelm, 2002; Snow, Burns, & Griffin, 1998; Wolfe, 2001). Some time during that wonderful year of teaching kindergarten, I saw a cartoon that depicted a small child stomping out of a school that showed a marquee reading, "First Day of Kindergarten." The child angrily says, "This will never work. I can't read. I can't write. And now, they won't let me talk." In many kindergarten classrooms, such restrictive learning structures remain all too true. The very way students learn best is curtailed. "I Used to Ask the Questions: Kindergartner's Lament" surfaced from concerns that some classroom routines may deprive children of their most comfortable and natural way to learn.

Reflection Questions

1. Recall a time when you were forced to learn something about which you had little or no interest. What thoughts and feelings did you have about that situation? Did you learn what you were expected to learn? What strategies did you employ to overcome your resistance? What would have made the situation more positive?

   _____

   _____

   _____

   _____

   _____

   _____

   _____

2. Think of two or three students in your classroom. What personal experiences, knowledge, and skills do they have? How can you capitalize on these areas in various learning situations?

   _____

   _____

   _____

   _____

   _____

   _____

   _____

3. While recognizing the importance of staying focused on goals and objectives, how can you still honor questions that can get teachers "off track"?

   _____

   _____

   _____

   _____

   _____

   _____

   _____

Extended Activity

With a grade-level or content-area colleague, analyze one teaching unit for elements that must remain teacher controlled and areas where more student control may be possible. What might that unit look like if students were given some control regarding topic, approach, or product selection?

_____

_____

_____

_____

_____

_____

_____

_____

_____

_____

_____

_____

_____

_____

_____

_____

_____

_____

_____

_____

_____

_____

_____

_____

_____

_____

_____

Museums of Their Souls

"That which we elect to surround ourselves with
becomes the archive of our experience and the museum of our soul."
Thomas Jefferson (1743–1826)

Sometimes a quote remains with you for reasons you don't know.
Such was the quote from Jefferson I read some time ago.
I pondered it for months it seems; it became a lens to see
All that encircled those I loved—those who meant the world to me.

And thus equipped, I went to school with daughter and with son
To view the archives they were building; the museums they'd begun.
I visited both rooms awhile and realized that day
The crucial roles a teacher's beliefs and temperament can play.

For...
Surrounding this gentle child of mine, whose little-girl ways delighted my heart
Was a shelf full of books beyond her grasp, and nothing nearby in which she could
    take part.
Desks isolated in rows wall to wall,
And a stagnated silence that smothered them all.
A chalkboard that named those who failed to mind,
Along with the check marks for how many times.
And a teacher—oh, a teacher who lectured and hushed,
Who assigned and assessed and made everyone rush.
She spewed out the facts, and the lessons she rambled;
Thus my daughter was left with an archive in shambles.

Yet...
Surrounding this gentle child of mine, whose little-boy ways filled my heart with joy
Were boxes of books of all sizes and levels, whose topics could interest a girl *and* a
    boy.
Tables designed to share questions and thoughts,
And the humming of learning that deep thinking brought.
A chalkboard that listed a message of praise,
Along with some rubrics and a poem for the day.
And a teacher—ah, a teacher who listened and cared,
Who modeled, encouraged, and helped them to dare.
Her manner and words made you sense that her goal
Was enriching the museum of my son's soul.

An archive that's meager; a museum that's full
Depends on the teacher who creates what is "school."
Some create rooms of heartache; some bring rooms alive.
Some cause children to wither; some help them to thrive.
Yet each student's right is to grow and to learn
In a climate of caring and genuine concern.
The duty's profound, and it should be so,
For teachers build "archives of experience," "museums of souls."

Background: Museums of Their Souls

I love quotes. I've collected them since I was a young girl. About five years ago, I came across the quote by Thomas Jefferson that became the framework for this poem. The content of the poem, however, stems from an incident that occurred many more years ago when I was privy to a conversation between a principal and two parents about placement. The parents had requested that their twins be placed in separate classrooms. There were only two classrooms at that particular grade level: One was stellar; the other, as the principal stated, was "one I'm reluctant to put any child in." Although there was not enough evidence of educational malpractice to terminate the offending teacher, administrators at the school and district levels feared that the differences between the negative, thwarting classroom and the positive, thriving classroom would become glaringly obvious when the twins shared their school-day experiences. The unfairness of the situation annoyed me for a long time. I tried to look at the situation as an administrator, as a teacher, and as a parent. None of the views looked good to me. I was reminded of Smith's (1986) statement:

> Learning is never divorced from feelings—and neither is failing to learn. We don't just learn about something, we simultaneously learn how we feel as we learn. Often the memory of the feeling lasts longer than the actual thing we learned. (p. 60)

I worried about what feelings about learning, about the subjects learned, and about herself as a learner the one child would garner that year. This travesty of subjecting some children to an inadequate educational experience inspired "Museums of Their Souls."

Reflection Questions

1. Recall your favorite teacher. What made him or her your favorite? Do any of the characteristics and qualities of that teacher, or the classroom environment he or she created, carry over into your own teaching? Why or why not?

_____

_____

_____

_____

_____

_____

2. Define the culture of the school in which you teach. List examples of how the school culture contributes to the environment of individual classrooms and the behaviors of teachers. Are there elements of your school culture that you feel are detrimental to positive learning experiences? If so, what could be done about those elements?

_____

_____

_____

_____

_____

_____

3. Summarize your beliefs about learners, learning, subject matter, and school in general. How do these beliefs influence the manner in which you conduct your classroom?

_____

_____

_____

_____

_____

_____

Extended Activity

Set up a video camera to record several hours in your classroom. This tape is for your use only, so select a typical day and do not plan anything special for this recording session. Review the recording and chart those behaviors, events, and environmental factors you would give as evidence to parents that their students are in a positive and caring learning community. Is your chart substantial or limited? How might you use this documentation to enhance the learning environment of your students?

_____

_____

_____

_____

_____

_____

_____

_____

_____

_____

_____

_____

_____

_____

_____

_____

_____

_____

_____

_____

_____

_____

_____

_____

The Feel of a Pencil

The computer is calling me.
I've a story to write.
I'll use the computer—of course...
It's faster.
It's better.
It spells and edits and prints out what I do.

The computer is nagging me.
I've a story to write.
Blank document's up; cursor's set to go.
Can't get started.
Can't begin.
The story is close to my heart and I can't hear the song.

The computer is harassing me.
I've a story to write.
Empty words fill a page; hollow paragraphs emerge.
Tapping the keys.
Scrolling through text.
I'm losing the very soul of what I want to say.

A pencil is whispering.
I've a story to write.
A point of lead beckons from where I sit.
It's old.
It's worn.
But I love the sound of graphite dancing over paper.

The computer is mute.
I've a story to write.
I hit Delete and embrace a trusted friend.
It glides.
It hums.
It pulls the hidden phrases from my heart.

A pencil is reassuring me.
I've a tale to write.
Smell of lead awakens all my senses.
I breathe.
I feel.
Words adorn each cherished page.

The computer is calling—
No doubt, will call again.
But when I struggle with what my heart is saying—
Ah, the feel of lead over vellum!
I reach for a pencil,
And then begin to sing.

Background: The Feel of a Pencil

When I was working as a literacy specialist, I visited a second-grade classroom during writers' workshop. One little girl was working diligently on her piece of writing, and I complimented her on her fine work. She smiled at me and with a sigh shared, "It would be an even better story if I could write it with purple marker. I write my best stories in purple marker because it makes writing more fun." I immediately empathized with this child because I, too, have my writing preference. If I'm writing something dear to my heart, I must write it first in pencil. In fact, the first draft of every poem in this collection was written in pencil. I enjoy the tactile experience of the lead gliding over paper, and somehow, the extra time it takes to form the words enables me to do a better job of teasing out the emerging thoughts and feelings. As Schlechty (1992) from the Center for Leadership in School Reform reminds us, students are volunteers, and although we can insist on their compliance, their commitment is under their control. He espouses the idea that commitment is more easily given when students are presented with quality work. Among the fundamental characteristics of that quality work are novelty and variety. Students should be asked to "use new skills, as well as new and different media, approaches, styles of presentation, and modes of analysis" (Schlechty, 1997, p. 17). How many children in the second-grade classroom I observed had writing preferences they were not encouraged to use? I wondered what other novel and varied learning approaches remained untapped. Thus, "The Feel of a Pencil" was born.

Reflection Questions

1. List your personal learning styles and preferences. How do they make themselves evident in your teaching and your classroom routines? What is their impact on your students?

   _____

   _____

   _____

   _____

   _____

   _____

   _____

2. Select three students at varying levels of academic success. What are their learning styles and preferences? Analyze the relationship among their learning styles and preferences, the characteristics of your classroom, and the level of their academic success. What does this analysis indicate?

   _____

   _____

   _____

   _____

   _____

   _____

   _____

3. Because it may not be possible to accommodate every learning style and preference in your classroom, brainstorm with a colleague what actions to take when students feel there is little choice in when, why, how, and what they are learning.

   _____

   _____

   _____

   _____

   _____

   _____

   _____

Extended Activity

Ask students to list some of their learning preferences (adapt the question to meet the appropriate developmental level of your students). Questions might include the following: Do you like to read by yourself or with a friend? Do you like to sit at a table to work or recline on the floor? Do you like complete silence when you are thinking or studying or do you like to have soft music in the background? For more ideas about students' learning preferences, refer to *Teaching Kids With Learning Difficulties in the Regular Classroom* (Winebrenner, 1996, p. 44) for a list of characteristics of analytical versus global thinkers. Use the student responses to graph the profile of your classroom learning preferences. What preferences are consistently met? Are there preferences that are not met?

Additional Resources About School Environment

Brownlie, F., Feniak, C., & Schnellert, L. (2006). *Student diversity: Classroom strategies to meet the learning needs of all students*. Portland, ME: Stenhouse.

Flint, A.S., & Riordan-Karlsson, M. (2001). *Buried treasures in the classroom: Using hidden influences to enhance literacy teaching and learning*. Newark, DE: International Reading Association.

Hoffman, D., & Levak, B. (2003). Personalizing schools. *Educational Leadership, 61*(1), 30–34.

Patterson, W. (2003). Breaking out of our boxes. *Phi Delta Kappan, 84*(8), 569–574.

Taylor, S., & Sobel, D. (2005). Creating classroom environments that are supportive of students' diverse backgrounds. *Colorado Reading Council Journal, 16*(2), 5–12.

Section II

REFLECTIONS ABOUT

CURRICULUM

"All genuine learning is active, not passive.
It involves the use of the mind, not just the memory.
It is a process of discovery, in which the student
is the main agent, not the teacher."

MORTIMER J. ADLER (1984, p. 50)

When Spelling Rules

I thought...

I had a most extraordinary day!

*I happ'ed upon this pulchritude of
nature in haphazard disarray:*

Myriad daffodils midst hyacinths of spring

Adorned a field nestled in a forest's opening.

*Though I had dates to keep and
commitments to fulfill,*

*Vistas before me awed my soul and
made my heart stand still.*

*I thought that this idyllic view could not
be more complete,*

*When doe with fawn wandered in
and dipped their heads to eat.*

*Overcome by such a view; I knew I
had to stay—*

*Few moments in my hectic life took
my breath away.*

*Hour elapsed within the span that seemed
just like a minute,*

*A cherished hour that now enclosed
a treasured memory in it.*

*The Keats I'd heard my teacher read
at last began to breathe:*

*"A thing of beauty is a joy forever."
At long last, I believe.*

I wrote...

I had a day experienced by few!

I came across this quiet, lovely view:

Various spring flowers were blowing
in the breeze,

And filled an open field in the middle
of the trees.

I had so much to do that day, had
people to receive,

But the scene before me was so nice,
I felt too moved to leave.

And though I thought this picture could
not be more a treat,

A doe and baby walked right in and
looked for food to eat.

So surprised to see all this, I knew I had
to wait—

A view like this was rare for me on such
a busy date.

I stayed an hour and couldn't believe that it
had passed so fast,

Leaving me with memories I know will always
last.

The Keats I'd heard my teacher read got
clearer to me somehow.

"A thing of beauty is a joy forever."
Is real to me now.

Background: When Spelling Rules

When I began my master's program, my instructor, Lynn K. Rhodes, shared with the class a story called "I Had a Cat." It was a poignant piece about a young, reluctant writer who refused to write anything. Finally, after much encouragement, she wrote "I had a cat." Delighted by this monumental progress, the teacher exclaimed, "Tell me more about your cat!" The child looked at her and replied, "I don't really have a cat, but I can spell 'I had a cat.'"

I've never forgotten that story—sadly, because I so often see it reenacted. Nearly all students have a more advanced speaking vocabulary than spelling vocabulary. At times, requiring students to be correct, even in the early stages of writing, inhibits their motivation to use the enriched speaking vocabularies they possess. Even when misspellings (i.e., invented, approximated, or temporary spellings) are allowed in early drafts, requiring every final piece of writing to be accurate in all conventions discourages novice writers who—usually on multiple occasions—must correct spelling and applications of punctuation and capitalization. We need to consider that whatever is done to promote better spellers should not simultaneously discourage writers! Frank Smith, author of *Writing and the Writer* (1994), states, "There is not much point in learning to spell if you have little intention of writing..." (p. 199). However, because accurate spelling remains a hallmark of being well educated, we still need to balance the demand for accuracy and the genuine need to express oneself in writing. As one fourth-grade student stated, "Invented spelling makes you feel that you have more than one hundred chests filled with words to choose from. You don't feel limited to only easier words" (as cited in Routman, 2000, p. 405). Quite recently, I observed a child who erased his misspelled attempt at writing *terrier* and replaced it with *dog*. It brought back memories of the "I Had a Cat" story and prompted "When Spelling Rules."

Reflection Questions

1. Even without the added pressure and demands of high-stakes tests, correct spelling and accurate use of other conventions of print are important. How do you balance demands for correctness with maintaining an atmosphere that encourages writers to use the more sophisticated oral language they possess?

   _____

   _____

   _____

   _____

   _____

   _____

2. Semantics are important. The term *invented spelling* seems to be used less frequently than the terms *temporary spelling* or *approximated spelling* (approximations). Why do you think that change has happened? Do those newer terms connote something different from the interpretation of invented spelling? Does it matter? Why or why not?

   _____

   _____

   _____

   _____

   _____

   _____

3. Discuss with a grade-level colleague why it is common to hear teachers complain that students (e.g., fourth grade and beyond) still do not use correct punctuation in their writing. Assume that the students have been taught these skills in each grade. What do you feel must be changed to remedy the situation?

   _____

   _____

   _____

   _____

   _____

   _____

Extended Activity

For 20–30 minutes, tape record a class discussion. Choose a topic that is open-ended (no "right" answers required!) and one about which students are enthusiastic (e.g., a recent field trip, a school sporting or drama event, a political or environmental issue). Analyze the tape for vocabulary you do not commonly see in the students' written work. Make a list of these words and share them with your class—with no names attached. Ask students why some of the more colorful, descriptive words they use in their oral language do not appear in their written work. Plan your next steps based on the responses the students give.

Chapter 14

In Chapter 14, Denali I read
Is called Mt. McKinley by all but a few;
At 20,320 feet one can get quite a view.

But my brother's book on ancients...
Said that Denali's the "home of the sun."
Formed by warriors with a battle to be won.
How the natives and locals revere it to this day,
And how some face the mountain whenever they pray.

In Chapter 14, the totems I saw
Exist in abundance along Ketchikan's shore;
No city elsewhere can boast of more.

But the museum in my grandma's town...
Had family stories of what totems mean;
Lavish abstracts in the color of dreams.
An old storyteller whispered low
A tale of what it was like long ago.

In Chapter 14, the climate I learned
Has temperature ranges that get extreme,
And seasons where daylight is only a dream.

But my father, who lived in Alaska, recalled...
There isn't a place where the sun's so strong,
And the flowers make up for the nights so long.
And the pristine beauty that is Glacier Bay's
Stays in your soul for the rest of your days.

In Chapter 14, the six questions it posed
Asked names of explorers and rivers and such;
The exports of Juneau; what towns
purchased what.

But Mother asked when she'd seen what I'd learned...
If I thought Alaska was the "last frontier"—
If I'd like to see a polar bear near—
If glacier walking would be fun to do—
If I'd ever race an Iditarod or two.

Chapter 14's read from beginning to end.
I've taken my notes; lots of time did I spend
Learning the names and the numbers and dates;
I'm ready as ever for the test that awaits.

Yet, I can't help but wonder...
I can't help but wish...
Oh, never mind;
No reason to dream...

The test is only on Chapter 14.

I recall a time when I was teaching fourth grade and the students took a published, multiple-choice test on a nonfiction article they had read in a weekly magazine. One of the mundane questions asked what color baby zebras are. The "correct" response was the item "black and white." One of my students approached me and said there was no right answer given among the choices for that question. When I asked him to explain, he said, "Well, I know they want me to say 'black and white,' but that's not really true. I saw baby zebras, and they are more dark brown and white when they are born." He continued to tell me quite a bit about zebras, and I realized the multiple-choice test was so inadequate. He knew so much more than he could ever show via the test's simplistic approach.

In *Student-Centered Classroom Assessment*, Stiggins (1996) discusses the caution teachers need to take whenever interpreting "objective" tests. We need to remember that, generally, test items represent a small part of the total domain of knowledge about a given topic. Although credible test-publishers—and teachers—strive to ensure that the test items chosen represent the significant understandings about the content, often more knowledge is *not* tested than is. In the assessment frenzy of today's educational milieu, it seems important to keep in mind that even the high-stakes tests—or, more accurately, *especially* the high-stakes tests—are measuring only part of what our students may or may not know and be able to do. Because the tests so often determine the curriculum, and the curriculum too often determines the resources offered, I thought of the limitations we put on learning when we restrict students to only one source of information and do not capitalize on the many kinds of resources available. How many of our bright students may be penalized because what *they* know is never the question asked. I recalled a unit test on Alaska and wrote "Chapter 14."

Reflection Questions

1. As part of your next unit or chapter test (regardless of content), allow students to list two or three concepts or skills that they know or are able to do that were not part of the assessment. Do their responses reflect significant learning? Why do you think they remembered those particular concepts or skills?

    _____

    _____

    _____

    _____

    _____

    _____

2. List the resources available for one of your units of study. How many different resources are there? How varied are they? How many are used by even your struggling students? Are any of the resources brought in by students? Are students a part of the process of resource selection?

    _____

    _____

    _____

    _____

    _____

    _____

3. When a school district or the curriculum dictates the use of a specific textbook, how can you extend the assessment of understanding beyond the content of the given text? How can you credit students for knowing more than the textbook assessment required?

    _____

    _____

    _____

    _____

    _____

    _____

Extended Activity

With a content-area or grade-level colleague, compare teacher-made classroom assessments that you both have administered to your students. At least part of the assessment should be selected response (e.g., true–false, multiple choice). If you already design assessments together, try to obtain a copy of a similar assessment from a colleague in a different school. What items are the same? Where do you differ? Discuss why you selected the items you did and omitted others. Would your students have scored better or worse on your colleague's assessment? What does this comparison reveal about the objectivity of tests?

Dearth of Dictionary Learning

When first you learn to use a dictionary,

You learn key words, and pronunciation marks.
You learn the roots of words, and where each one began;
How they changed from Old to Middle English,
Or the metamorphoses past-tense spelling can demand.

You learn where to find what part of speech applies just when,
And plural rules, and all the rules' exceptions.
And, of course, you learn the meaning of each utterance
That's so neatly compiled in alphabetized selection.

But you don't learn what matters.

You learn a word, but you don't learn its story.
You don't learn what made each declaration come alive.
You don't see the face of who first coined expressions,
Or know when or why or how they felt inside.

Did it hurt to first cry "war" from an embattled mouth?
Did the soldier sense with ghastly, tortured gaze
That words like *hate* and *death* and *cold betrayal*
Would cut more deeply than the sword he raised?

Did someone sigh when she first uttered "beauty"?
Did a mother weep when "baby" was first spoken?
Did music fill the air with the first "I love you"?
Or did someone die when he first said his "heart was broken"?

Was "friendship" said in tandem by both people?
Or hallowed by the giver of the two?
Was "thief" or "robber" spat out first by victims?
Or declared by culprits as they stealthily withdrew?

Yes, when you learn to use a dictionary,

You learn useful information about words.
Yet if a deeper understanding is not found,
You'll lack the soul and spirit and very marrow
That put life in words and flesh on thought to sound.

If facts alone are what you do remember,
Emptiness will be what that will cost.
You'll leave your mind and heart and very being
To yearn for faces gone, and stories lost.

Background: Dearth of Dictionary Learning

When I taught fourth grade, I used to present a "word of the week." The choice was somewhat random—a word I came across in my own reading that I thought the students would find interesting (e.g., *chagrined*), a word that was fun to say (e.g., *pithy*), or a word that had an intriguing history (e.g., *mnemonic*). On the weekly Friday spelling test, the students were encouraged to try the word—both to spell it and to define it. Students did not lose points if they misspelled the word, nor did they get extra credit if they were correct. This was strictly "for fun." I always was amazed how many students tried the word, and how many consistently got it right. This observation led to two musings: First, the power of just enjoying words and, second, the freedom and motivation to learn when consequences were removed.

In *Words Their Way: Word Study for Phonics, Vocabulary, and Spelling Instruction*, Bear, Invernizzi, Templeton, and Johnston (1996) illustrate that examining the history of the English language presents a "wonderful and instructive terrain that our students—and *we*—can explore" (p. 28). Kohn (1993) reminds us that we are "beings who possess natural curiosity about ourselves and our environment, who search for and overcome challenges, who try to master skills and attain competence, and who seek to reach new levels of complexity in what we learn and do" (p. 25)—without the necessity of external rewards or punishment. The intriguing story of words and the lack of any form of repercussion did indeed make my students avid word researchers. One student took his interest even further when he approached me one afternoon and asked, "Mrs. Durica, I get that the word came from the Greek language, but who *said the word first?*" Ever since that query, I've thought about the people in the stories behind words. These stories enliven the study of the English language and transform dull and laborious lessons about grammar, spelling, and definitions into exciting quests for meaning. My recorded thoughts became "Dearth of Dictionary Learning."

Reflection Questions

1. Tackle this rarely asked question: What is your favorite word? Think about it. What is a word you like to say because it feels good in your mouth, or it evokes a certain feeling or memory, or it is just so very useful? Write about why you have selected that word. Share your writing with your colleagues and then with your students. Ask them to think about their favorite word and share it (either orally or in writing) with a peer. (Note: This particular reflection, though seemingly light-hearted, has provoked more profound and interesting discussions in my classes than many of the more "weighted" prompts. Take it seriously and give it a try.)

    _____

    _____

    _____

    _____

2. Researchers note that the teacher's enthusiasm for words influences the vocabulary and spelling achievement of his or her students (Bear et al., 1996; Gentry & Gillet, 1993). How do you share your interest in words with your students? How does your own enthusiasm for language influence your students' motivation?

    _____

    _____

    _____

    _____

3. Grades can be a form of praise or punishment. List the reasons why you think grades contribute to learning. List the reasons why you think grades inhibit learning. Do you think grades do more to enhance or to inhibit the joy and necessary risk-taking of learning? Hypothesize what the learning atmosphere in your classroom would be like if no grades were given for certain tasks or assignments. How would it be different?

    _____

    _____

    _____

    _____

Extended Activity

With a small group of colleagues, explore the following statement from *Punished by Rewards: The Trouble With Gold Stars, Incentive Plans, A's, Praise, and Other Bribes* (Kohn, 1993): "The troubling truth is that rewards and punishments are not opposites at all; they are two sides of the same coin. And it is a coin that does not buy very much" (p. 50). Do you agree with that statement? How do you see that statement applying to the reward and punishment system you use in your classroom?

_____

_____

_____

_____

_____

_____

_____

_____

_____

_____

_____

_____

_____

_____

_____

_____

_____

_____

_____

_____

_____

_____

_____

I Read It Because It's Beautiful

Somehow a life without poetry seems...
 Dismal
  Empty
   Flat—
    Not much.

So each day in my classroom I read...
 Sonnets
  Haikus
   Free verse—
    And such.

An observer sat in my room one day...
 Noted poem's title
  Evaluated delivery
   Recorded "lesson" sequence—
    Said dryly: "It seems

There's no connection curricular-wise...
 No anticipatory set
  No vocabulary drill
   No comprehension query—
    Do they know what it means?"

I could have contrived a defense or two, but...
 Spirits flowed with peaceful joy
  Honesty prevailed
   Simple truth explained—
    "I read it because it's beautiful," I said.

She didn't quite frown but recalled all the same, "We've...
 Standards to meet
  Timelines to keep
   Pages to cover—
    Important content to be read."

I looked from her to my students' gaze; they...
 Had relished the words
  Danced with the rhythm
   Mused with the meaning—
    Were richer in spirit than when we began.

I read it because it was beautiful. And beauty is...
 Never superfluous
  Never irrelevant
   Always needed—
    Always in my "lesson" plan.

Background: I Read It Because It's Beautiful

No matter what grade level I taught, I *did* begin each day with a poem. It grounded us somehow to come together and experience language (no matter how briefly) and to discuss—with no right or wrong answers—ideas. Often the poetry I selected did correlate with topics we were studying, or approaching holidays, or the season of the year. Yet, sometimes, just for the pure beauty of the words and rhythm of the lines, I shared a poem that had nothing to do with anything. It simply was beautiful. One day, the supervisor of a preservice teacher whom I was mentoring visited my classroom. I began the day with the usual poem, reread it because it was indeed so lovely, and then moved on to the day's lessons. The preservice teacher later told me that her supervisor commented that if I were not "going to do anything" with that poem, I should not have shared it. Time was too precious to waste! I thought about that comment for a long time. I remembered the time my first graders, on their own, began clapping the rhythm of the horses' hooves the day I shared Henry Wadsworth Longfellow's "Paul Revere's Ride" (1971). I remembered when one of my students looked at a flock of Canadian honkers flying overhead and said, "Look! Something told the wild geese it was time to fly!"—the refrain of a poem by Rachel Field (1971) that I had read to the class weeks earlier. Those and other memories affirmed that I not only did not waste time—I had enhanced it! Although the poems struck particular students differently, all the poems seemed to bring us together through the language we shared. They helped us to connect to our world and to one another. Darling-Hammond (1997) states that "reaching every student rather than covering curriculum, connecting to all learners rather than merely offering education, is our task" (p. 43). Taking a brief break from the implementation of the established curriculum seemed a small price to pay for relishing our language and connecting us as a community of learners. To me, that made poetry essential. That belief is reflected in "I Read It Because It's Beautiful."

Reflection Questions

1. Do your students sense that they are a community of learners? What evidence is there to support your response? Do you think being a community is important to your students' academic achievement? If so, what steps can be taken to build or to strengthen that community?

   _____

   _____

   _____

   _____

   _____

   _____

2. Other than curriculum-based instruction, list any other activities in which students engage during a given day or class period. Prioritize that list in order of importance to learning. Are any activities "wasted time"? Would an outside observer think you are not using time wisely? How would you explain some of the activities to someone who questions their value?

   _____

   _____

   _____

   _____

   _____

   _____

3. Ask your students to jot down their favorite part of the class period or of the day (when they are in the classroom—this time recess or lunch doesn't count!) and to list some reasons why they selected that particular time. What do you notice about their responses? Can this data be used to enhance student commitment to and ownership of their learning?

   _____

   _____

   _____

   _____

   _____

   _____

Extended Activity

Curriculum consultant Allan Glatthorn (1994) offers as a general rule that only 60%–75% of time should be spent on the mastery curriculum—that is, the knowledge and set of skills essential for all students to master and on which they are likely to be tested:

> This approach leaves sufficient time for...teams to develop an enrichment curriculum for all students and provides some limited time for student-determined [curriculum]. (Note the irony of present practice: schools offer an enrichment curriculum to those who least need it—the gifted—and deny it to those who could best profit from it—the at-risk.) (p. 29)

With your content-area and grade-level colleagues, analyze the amount of time each day or week that is spent on prescribed curriculum. Do you think your students would benefit from having time to pursue interests or topics outside of that curriculum? How much, if any, time should be allotted for such endeavors? Describe what the instructional day might look like with such changes.

_____

_____

_____

_____

_____

_____

_____

_____

_____

_____

_____

_____

_____

_____

_____

_____

_____

_____

_____

Additional Resources About Curriculum

Allington, R. (2002). What I've learned about effective reading instruction: From a decade of studying exemplary elementary classroom teachers. *Phi Delta Kappan, 83*(10), 740–747.

Clinchy, E. (1999). *Reforming American education: From the bottom to the top.* Portsmouth, NH: Heinemann.

Cohen, D., & Ball, D. (2001). Making change: Instruction and its improvement. *Phi Delta Kappan, 83*(1), 73–77.

Cunningham, P., & Allington, R. (2003). *Classrooms that work: They can all read and write* (3rd ed.). Boston: Allyn & Bacon.

Scherer, M. (2002). Do students care about learning? A conversation with Mihaly Csikszentmihalyi. *Educational Leadership, 60*(1), 12–17.

Section III

REFLECTIONS ABOUT

DIVERSITY
IN THE
CLASSROOM

"To be nobody but yourself—in a world which is doing its best, night and day, to make you everybody else—means to fight the hardest battle which any human being can fight; and never stop fighting."

E.E. CUMMINGS, U.S. POET, PAINTER, ESSAYIST, AND PLAYWRIGHT (1894–1962)

The Labeled Child

I pray for the labeled child—
That child who is gifted and talented.
No longer can she be carefree and
    idle,
Or a daydreamer.
So much more is expected
Of those as gifted and talented as she.

I pray for the labeled child—
That child who is learning disabled.
No longer will the world expect
    brilliance.
No longer will someone tell him to reach
    for the stars
Because that is where greatness will be
    found.

I pray for the labeled child—
That child who is dyslexic.
Reading—oh, the joy of reading—
Will always be hard for her to find.
No matter that she can recite—no,
    sing!—
Mary Had a Little Lamb,
She won't be able to read it.
At least not without difficulty.
She will learn that all her friends
Who laugh and cry and wonder about
    books
Can do so because they are not dyslexic.

I pray for the labeled child—
That child who is ADHD.
An unorganized bubble of hyperactivity.
No longer will someone teach him to
    cope
In a world that values compliance.
No longer will someone say,
"You can do this;
Oh it may be hard, but it is within you to
    do this."
An automatic dose of medication now
    replaces the need for inner effort,
And eliminates the possible victory.

I pray for the labeled child—
That child who is emotionally
    handicapped.
That child who rebels
Because she *should* rebel.
The child who acts out
Because there is nowhere else
For the hurt and anxiety and fear to go.
The child who is diagnosed "sick,"
When perhaps her actions are the one
    true sign of sanity
In the demented world in which she is
    forced to live.

I pray for the child of no label.
In a system which marks so many special,
This child neither shines nor demands.
For this child, life has been neither harsh
    nor generous.
This is the one who "makes" the
    teacher's day
Because there are so many children who
    need *real* attention.

I pray most of all for some magic day
When the tests, the labels, and the names
Will disappear—will be forgotten.
When each child who enters a classroom
Will be an apprentice of learning.
When each classroom will be a safe
    haven
To discover—on your own—
What will be the struggles of your life,
And the victories.
When the frail and the bright,
The gregarious and the shy
Will all find their place
In the great adventure of education.
When the only label that will be attached
    to anyone is
        LEARNER.

Background: The Labeled Child

The events that prompted this poem transpired over a month's time. I was teaching in an elementary school, and on different occasions I heard teachers talking about their students by a given label. It shocked me. Brian wasn't Brian; he was "my G/T [gifted and talented] kid." Carrie wasn't Carrie; she was "my SPED [special education] kid." It seemed to be an epidemic. Suddenly, students had no names–just labels. The final and most appalling occurrence was when a teacher introduced me to a little boy as "my ADHD [attention deficit hyperactivity disorder] kid" with the child standing right in front of her! I had studied the impact of teacher expectation on students, and I worried about the influence such stereotypical thinking had on the instruction of these teachers, let alone on their relationships with their students. I remembered that the "Pygmalion Study" of the 1960s (Winebrenner, 1996) demonstrated that students improved dramatically when their teachers had been told that they had done extremely well in the previous year and were at an intellectual peak for learning. Because of technical difficulties with the research, that particular study experienced criticism in subsequent years; yet, more recent investigations into teacher expectation have confirmed that student achievement is indeed influenced by teacher expectations (Brophy, 1983; Cooper & Good, 1983; Good, 1987). Researchers such as Cotton (2006) have noted the differential treatment stemming from teacher expectation, both toward individual students and toward different ability groups within classrooms. For example, those students "in low groups or tracks have been found to get less exciting instruction, less emphasis upon meaning and conceptualization, and more rote drill and practice activities" (¶ 36). I also have found the same to be true in many classrooms in which I observed the instruction given to the high group versus that of the low group. The obvious differences in expectations and rigor verify why the low group tends to remain such forever. Few phenomena in education concern me as much as how we so readily label our children. "The Labeled Child" arose from the utter unfairness these labels are to our students' uniqueness—to the strengths and the needs our simplistic labels fail to recognize.

Reflection Questions

1. How does the extensive research regarding the relation between teacher expectation and student achievement apply to the typical labels students are given in schools? How does it directly apply to your students?

   _____

   _____

   _____

   _____

   _____

   _____

2. Do you prefer to know a lot about your students before the first day of school, or do you prefer to wait until you have formed your own impression before delving into their files? Are there advantages to either approach? What are they? What might be the disadvantages?

   _____

   _____

   _____

   _____

   _____

   _____

3. Think of a student with whom you work who has a label (e.g., G/T, SPED, ADHD, ELL [English-language learner]). Reflect on how that label may influence your interactions with that student and his or her family. Speculate about what might change if tomorrow you found out that that label was no longer a valid designation for that student.

   _____

   _____

   _____

   _____

   _____

   _____

Extended Activity

For one week, raise your level of consciousness about the frequency with which labels are used regarding both colleagues and students. As you hear conversations in the teachers' lounge, comments in the halls, or dialogues with parents on the playground or in the office, what sets of behaviors, personality traits, or abilities are being condensed into a "convenient label"? Make a list of the labels you have heard. Have those labels added to or detracted from your understanding of those individuals?

_____

_____

_____

_____

_____

_____

_____

_____

_____

_____

_____

_____

_____

_____

_____

_____

_____

_____

_____

_____

_____

_____

_____

_____

_____

_____

My Friend's G/T

My friend's a gifted student;
He's talented, you know.
He goes to a special classroom
With a sign that tells him so.

The sign hangs by the doorway.
It says: "G/T enter here."
You don't go in if you're not bright;
The sign makes that quite clear.

My friend once took a test in math
And a test in English too,
That marked him as a gifted kid
Who could do more than I can do.

I asked to take the test to see
If I could join my friend,
But the teacher said my average grades
Foretold the story's end.

So each day I pass his classroom
And view what smart kids learn,
And wonder if *my* questions
Are anyone's concern.

One question that I ponder
And think about a lot...
If that sign tells him he's gifted,
Is it telling me I'm not?

Background: My Friend's G/T

While working as a teacher in the late 1980s, I decided to place a sign above my classroom door that read "Class for the Gifted and Talented." I was a firm believer in Gardner's theory of multiple intelligences (1983), which suggests that there is no general intelligence but rather multiple, individual intelligences. He maintains that these separate and distinct components to intelligence influence our interests, exhibit themselves in our talents and preferences, and may have an impact on the ease with which we learn certain types of material. I delighted in recognizing the many ways in which my students shone, and I searched for opportunities where their varied talents and abilities could be tapped. Differentiating some instructional approaches as well as allowing more choice in how final products were presented brought new life into my classroom. It was not uncommon for struggling students to be as motivated as those who had seemed more advanced. Erwin's (2004) comment about motivation explains this concept: "The truth is that *all* students are motivated, but they may not be motivated to learn and behave in ways that teachers and schools [traditionally] prefer" (p. 23). I did realize that it was not because of the sign, but because of the changes I made, that my class developed into a rejuvenated community of learners—a community about which that sign could not have been more true. However, it did not take long before an assistant principal meekly asked me to take down my sign, as parents of the *identified* gifted and talented students might object to my stating that *everyone* was gifted and talented. That was not an issue I was ready to take on that year; I had other battles I was fighting. However, I have always regretted taking down that sign. With well-deserved recognition and praise for students who are identified as gifted and talented, I can't help but wonder what that statement says to the other students in our schools. When a middle school student told me one day that she wouldn't be in the same class as her best friend because her best friend was "much smarter" than she was—"she's gifted, you know"—I was really hit with the impact of just what that label does for those who have it, and for those who don't. "My Friend's G/T" was written to recognize both.

Reflection Questions

1. Tomlinson (1999), a leading authority on differentiation, states, "Many current understandings about learning provide strong support for classrooms that recognize, honor, and cultivate individuality" (p. 18). How do you recognize the individual and varied gifts and talents of all your students, so that each has an arena in which he or she can shine?

   _____

   _____

   _____

   _____

   _____

   _____

2. A 1995 study by Jaeger and Hattie concludes, "On the average, the achievement effect of ability grouping is quite small, equaling less than one-fifth of a standard deviation in student achievement" (p. 219). When do you think it *is* appropriate to group by ability? Why? What benefits for the students do you have as evidence that ability grouping is a positive experience for them? Is it as positive regardless of the group they are in?

   _____

   _____

   _____

   _____

   _____

   _____

3. Ask some students identified as gifted and talented what they like best about their school experience. Do their responses have any implications for your classroom instruction?

   _____

   _____

   _____

   _____

   _____

   _____

Extended Activity

If opportunity allows, observe the instruction delivered to a group of identified gifted and talented students. If this is not possible, arrange for an interview with a teacher who teaches children identified as gifted and talented. Note the characteristics of that instruction (i.e., the kinds of questions asked, the wait-time given, the types of resources used, the amount of student versus teacher talking, the degree of student choice, and so forth). Chart the similarities and differences in the instruction you observe (or hear about) and the instruction found in typical classrooms. With a content-area or grade-level colleague, discuss your findings and what implications they may have for your own instruction.

_____

_____

_____

_____

_____

_____

_____

_____

_____

_____

_____

_____

_____

_____

_____

_____

_____

_____

_____

_____

_____

_____

I'm Partially Proficient

I held the schools accountable for teaching what schools should teach.
So when state assessments first began
I was anxious as the next to see where my son's school would stand.

My son's so bright, you know.
I marvel every day at his detailed observations of life—
His insights into everything from the cranky old neighbor across the street
   to the complexities of global strife.

He's so full of life, my son.
His laughter shatters the gloomiest day,
Warms the hardest of hearts, and lightens the burdens that come my way.

He's an avid reader, you know, my son.
Lazy Saturdays include sharing Garfield cartoons
And basketball stats pepper Sunday afternoons.

He's never cared much for writing, my son.
But letters to his uncle keep squadron spirits alive,
And are kept close at heart till the next one arrives.

He's a kind boy, my son.
Oh, he quibbles with friends, and sometimes he's cross,
But he tears at sad movies if children aren't loved and his heart nearly breaks
   over pets that are lost.

He's all I could ever want in a son.
Since his birth my life has been joy beyond measure.
He is a gift—beautiful, and treasured.

But today, I stopped caring about state assessments, school ranking
   or accountability.
My son, my gift, my treasure, in a broken voice, announced when he
   came home:
"I'm partially proficient, Mom."

Background: I'm Partially Proficient

Since I began my career in education, school districts have used labels (e.g., G/T, ELL, SPED) to classify students, although the acronyms may have changed slightly over the years. With the more recent national movement to hold students accountable for attaining specific academic standards and the subsequent proficiency tests, state governments also are contributing to the labeling of our children. In the state in which I reside and have worked, Colorado, the labels include *advanced*, *proficient*, *partially proficient*, and *unsatisfactory*. Although the National Research Council's report "High Stakes: Testing for Tracking, Promotion and Graduation" (Heubert & Hauser, 1999) reiterates that "high-stakes educational decisions should not be made solely or automatically on the basis of a single test score but should also take other relevant information into account" (p. 6), the reality of the situation is that making decisions based solely on test scores is exactly what is happening in far too many places. Not only are entire schools graded based on how students performed on the state assessments, but I also have observed in schools where children have been grouped for instruction based on their state assessment scores. Furthermore, teachers who feel pressured to raise test scores "have a tendency to narrow the curriculum and inflate the importance of the test" (International Reading Association [IRA], 1999, n.p.), depriving students of deeper and broader understandings for the sake of drilling specific test elements.

As dispiriting as many of these consequences from the abuse of high-stakes testing can be, nothing was more discouraging to me than the day a parent shared with me that his son was deemed "partially proficient." The father had always thought his son was such a wonderful writer; he just couldn't believe that he was only "partially proficient." He said his son had been brokenhearted when he received his ranking. There are many ways to handle an incident such as this to help both the student and the parent understand the partially proficient category, but what hit me like a splash of cold water in my face was the impact those two words had had on the child and on his father. My concern about yet another label inspired "I'm Partially Proficient."

Reflection Questions

1. In its 1999 position statement about high-stakes assessments in reading, the IRA recommends that teachers "inform parents and the public about tests and their results" (n.p.). What *specific* steps have you taken to help parents—and most important, *students*—understand that the categories of the test scores depict the performance on one given test and do not describe the student? Have these actions been adequate? What else may need to be done to ensure that parents and students do not use state assessments (or any other evaluations) to label their children or themselves as a certain level of learner?

    _____

    _____

    _____

    _____

2. A 1997 position statement from the National Association for the Education of Young Children (NAEYC) proposes that assessments appropriate for primary-grade children rely "heavily on the results of observations...descriptive data, collections of representative work...and demonstrations of performance during authentic, not contrived, activities" (p. 14). If you are a primary-grade teacher, compare the assessments given to your students with the suggested forms of assessment listed above. If you are a middle school or secondary teacher, what roles do those types of assessment play in your students' evaluation portfolios?

    _____

    _____

    _____

    _____

3. Are labels (categories) used in your evaluation as a teacher or administrator? How has that made you feel? What might that tell you about helping students overcome less than desirable categorizations?

    _____

    _____

    _____

    _____

Extended Activity

Few schools have escaped the impact of statewide assessments. With a content-area or grade-level colleague, list the changes in instructional time and approach, as well as in available resources, that have occurred since high-stakes state testing has been implemented at your school. What changes have improved the educational climate? What changes have limited learning? What changes are the most challenging for you as the classroom teacher? Has this analysis provided information that encourages you to make additional changes?

_____

_____

_____

_____

_____

_____

_____

_____

_____

_____

_____

_____

_____

_____

_____

_____

_____

_____

_____

_____

_____

_____

_____

Unloved Stories:
A Poem for Two Voices

I can write, Mrs. Withers!

Of course you can, Jon.

I know lots about tigers,
   And spiders and gore;
I know all about fishing
   And monsters and war...

*Yes, Jon, but surely you know
so much more.*

Well, I know about aliens;
I know how they scream...

*But Jon, tell me this:
what is your DREAM?*

I dream about beating Zach Feld in a race,
And being like Superman,
And flying through space...

*But what does the rain
feel like on your face?*

The rain's only fun if it makes lots of mud.
I love when my shoes get all stuck in brown crud.

*Crud's not a word you
should use when you write.
Now, write a spring poem
how rain makes things all bright.*

OK, Mrs. Withers.

*Well...
Start...
Jon...BEGIN!*

I don't think I can write with this kind of pen.

Background:
Unloved Stories: A Poem for Two Voices

Although gender is not commonly thought of as a label, the practice of disaggregating test data has highlighted consistent gaps between the achievement of girls and boys, particularly in measures of mathematics, reading, and writing. Great strides have been made in closing the mathematical chasm, but literacy achievement data indicate that reading, and especially writing, remain a challenge for many male students (Brozo, 2002; Durica, 2004; Millard, 1997; Newkirk, 2002; Sadker, 2002; Smith & Wilhelm, 2002). In 2003, I had the opportunity to participate in Level II of the Colorado Writing Project, which bases its program on the same principles as the National Writing Project—including a focus on improving the teaching of writing by engaging *teachers* in writing. During that experience, I pursued the topic of why boys appear to be less successful than girls in standardized measures of writing. Two reoccurring messages in the many studies that I examined (Armon, 2003; Bauer, 2001; Ezarik, 2003; Goldberg & Roswell, 2003; Guzzetti, Young, Gritsavage, Fyfe, & Hardenbrook, 2002; Millard, 1997; Mulac & Lundell, 1994; Newkirk, 2002; Peterson, 2002; Smith & Wilhelm, 2002) were (1) the need for boys to feel that the stories they bring are as worthy as those topics selected by girls and (2) the importance of boys maintaining a sense of control over their writing.

I thought of some of the boys I taught, as well as observed, who were continually frustrated with writing. What they wrote was never "good enough" for their teachers or their parents. The words they chose were never the "right" ones. The parts of their stories that their teachers or parents told them to leave out were always the parts they liked the best. I recalled one incident a teacher shared with me involving a fourth-grade student whose mother happened to be helping in the classroom that day. She reprimanded him when the story he read aloud to the class was not as "nice" as the other stories she heard the children share. She called the teacher that evening and assured her: "Don't worry, my son will never write a story like that again!" Sadly, he won't—not after his mother's reproach and feedback. As I continue to investigate findings on this topic, I am gaining an even deeper understanding of the complexity of the issue and the critical need for teachers to honor what literacy interests and skills boys—and girls as well—bring to the writing table. "Unloved Stories: A Poem for Two Voices" not only summarizes my research findings but also illustrates my experiences with existing attitudes about classroom writing.

Reflection Questions

1. "Literary elitism" (Barrs & Pidgeon, 2003) is a theory that suggests that some books and topics are worthier of attention than others. Due to the expectations of the traditional curriculum, or their own personal preferences, teachers often select novels and writing topics that may not interest typical boys. This perpetuates the idea many male students hold about literacy being "a girl thing." With a colleague, brainstorm actions that can be taken to assure boys that some of their preferences (e.g., cartoons, how-to books, fantasy, action stories) are as worthwhile to read and write about as the teacher's selection.

   _____

   _____

   _____

   _____

   _____

2. In this age of increased responsibility regarding indications of violent behavior, how do you handle the proclivity male students have toward writing more action-oriented, violent pieces (Newkirk, 2002)? How can you establish necessary boundaries without implying that the topic selection is not a worthwhile piece? Share your ideas with a grade-level colleague.

   _____

   _____

   _____

   _____

   _____

3. How do you balance giving students a choice in writing and requiring them to write to certain prompts, or in certain structures? Are there particular elements of writing instruction where choice is more important than at other times?

   _____

   _____

   _____

   _____

   _____

Extended Activity

Thomas Newkirk, Jeffrey Wilhelm, Michael Smith, and William Brozo are among numerous researchers who have investigated the issue of boys and literacy achievement. Select one of these researchers (or any other researcher of the topic) and read one chapter of your choosing from his or her work. What insights from the researcher's work with boys help you to better match your instruction to the interests and needs of all of your students?

_____

_____

_____

_____

_____

_____

_____

_____

_____

_____

_____

_____

_____

_____

_____

_____

_____

_____

_____

_____

_____

_____

_____

Additional Resources About Diversity in the Classroom

Armstrong, T. (1994). *Multiple intelligences in the classroom*. Alexandria, VA: Association for Supervision and Curriculum Development.

Duffy, G., & Hoffman, J. (1999). In pursuit of an illusion: The flawed search for a perfect method. *The Reading Teacher, 53*, 10–16.

Page, S. (2000). When changes for the gifted spur differentiation for all. *Educational Leadership, 58*(1), 62–65.

Risko, V., & Bromley, K. (Eds.). (2001). *Collaboration for diverse learners: Viewpoints and practices*. Newark, DE: International Reading Association.

Strong, R., Silver, H., & Perini, M. (2001). Making students as important as standards. *Educational Leadership, 59*(3), 56–61.

Section IV

REFLECTIONS ABOUT

THE IMPACT OF
TEACHERS
AND PARENTS

"In a completely rational society...the best of us would aspire to be teachers, and the rest of us would have to settle for something less. Passing one generation to the next ought to be the highest responsibility and the highest honor anyone could have."

LIDO ANTHONY "LEE" IACOCCA,
FORMER CHAIRMAN OF CHRYSLER CORPORATION

The Man Who Let Me Speak

I came to school unable to do many things
That teachers—and my folks—thought counted most.
I struggled with my math and science projects,
And reading was a hardship; writing worse.

But once a week, I met with Mr. Foster.
Then, I spoke with ease and with accomplished grace.
For the language that he spoke would touch my
    heartstrings,
And I relished being in such safe a place.

His lessons always had some information,
But mostly we would practice what he preached.
And with him I was gifted as my classmates
Who could read, and write, and win awards in speech.

My time with him each week was like a treasure.
He loved to teach; and I...I loved to learn.
His passion for his topic made it easy;
My success appeared to be his first concern.

He'd orchestrate a chorus of varied learners:
Some sad, some joyful; those who seemed so bright.
And the harmony that echoed from his classroom
Enriched not just my day, but my whole life.

Mr. Foster was my music teacher.
His memory I cherish till this day.
He saw a talent others did not value,
And when I had no words, he let me play.

Background: The Man Who Let Me Speak

The arts are significant to many children whose abilities are in music, or drama, or graphic art. For example, I was headed for the photocopier one day when I passed a girl who was sitting in the office, waiting in line to see the principal. She had misbehaved in class and was waiting to be disciplined. She asked the secretary how much longer it would be before the principal was ready to see her. Her concern was that she was missing art—her favorite class. She told the secretary that it was the only class that she was the best student in. I thought about the recent trend in education to make classes like art, music, physical education, or theater second-class courses. Certainly, when budgets get tight, these courses often are the first to be cut. But what about those students who wait all day for that one class in which they can shine? What about that girl who was missing the only class she was "the best student in"? Although I understood the importance of students realizing that there are consequences for their actions, it still seemed ironic to me that this student was missing the one opportunity in the school day when her feelings of competency were likely to motivate her to behave well.

As I continued thinking about this, my contemplation expanded from just teachers of the arts to *all* teachers. As educators, we have the power and the responsibility to ensure that our students have the opportunity to shine. Whether we teach physics or finger painting, math or music, literature or line dancing, we need to look for opportunities to make our students feel competent. Granted, all students will not achieve the same level of competency in all areas, but they should leave our classes having had their moment in the spotlight. I remember when my older son started high school and the principal cautioned parents about immediately pulling their children from sports if their grades were not where they should be. He reminded us that if students can get involved in something they love to do, their feelings of competency and enthusiasm often trickle into other areas of their schooling experience. My experiences have shown me that that is true more often than not. The need to feel competent, and the rewards that brings, seems as necessary to life as food itself. The power we have as teachers in that journey toward competency is awesome indeed. I wrote "The Man Who Let Me Speak" to honor teachers who recognize their responsibility in helping students to shine.

Reflection Questions

1. Prioritize the abilities your school values. Compare your list with that of a colleague. Are they similar? Do you think all abilities are valued equally? Should they be? Why or why not? Which abilities do *you* most value? How does that influence your instruction and interaction with your students?

    _____

    _____

    _____

    _____

    _____

    _____

2. Gardner (1983) proposes that we ask not how intelligent are you, but how are you intelligent. Pose that question to your students. Analyze their responses. What does this information indicate about the concepts your students have about themselves as learners?

    _____

    _____

    _____

    _____

    _____

    _____

3. If students need to be pulled out of class for some event (e.g., special assistance, medical appointments) do you encourage them to miss certain classes rather than others? Why? Which classes would your students choose to miss if they were given the option? Ask them why they would make that choice. What do their responses tell you about their feelings of competency?

    _____

    _____

    _____

    _____

    _____

    _____

Extended Activity

Spend some time researching the concept of multiple intelligences. You should find not only explanations of the theory but also articles both supporting and questioning its basis. Collect the information and then share your findings with a colleague. After your discussion, craft a belief statement about your stance on the issue. Revisit your statement at the end of the school year. Is your statement still a valid representation of your thinking, or does it need to be altered? What confirmed your thinking or caused it to change?

The Bully

School was a dreadful place for me.
He was there every day.
Loomed over me;
Made me feel small
No matter how I tried to please.

He delighted in my embarrassment.
Pointed out my flaws;
Gave little or no care
Of who might hear my limitations
Or see me wince at his words.

He oppressed me with his power.
Daily made sure
I knew my place,
And had no illusions
Of moving into the accepted crowd.

I ached for his approval.
He gave it to a favored few.
I was tormented knowing
I never shone in any way
But in his disappointment.

I could not retaliate.
My impotence was guaranteed.
He was bigger than I;
Older than I;
Smarter than I.
He was my teacher.

Background: The Bully

So many of the teachers with whom I work tell me that they chose to teach because they want to make a difference in the lives of young people. They care, and they consider teaching to be a privilege. Shelley Harwayne (1999), former principal of The Manhattan New School, considers as an absolute necessity in any teachers she hires that they "consider it a privilege to be around children" (p. 5). Yet education, like all professions, has members who are shining examples of all that is good and laudable about teaching and members who are disappointments. For example, I had the opportunity to observe a high school algebra class that included several students who were repeating the course. One day, as the teacher returned the latest unit exam, he approached one particular student. The teacher literally threw the test paper on the student's desk, and in front of the entire class he announced, "Looks like you're going to flunk the second time around, too." I was horrified. I watched the dejected young man crumple the test into a ball and listlessly pitch it into a nearby trashcan—along with his hopes, his efforts, and his self-esteem. I immediately thought of the quote from the English historian Lord Acton: "Power tends to corrupt and absolute power corrupts absolutely" (Acton, 1948, p. 364). This was the ultimate example of the abuse of power! Here was a teacher who, for whatever reason, did not recognize his profound responsibility and the lasting impact his words would have on his students. In *The High-Performing Teacher*, Canter and Canter (1994) remind teachers that they "have the most important job in America today" (p. 3). An easy job? No. An important and influential job? Yes. Our students deserve that we live up to that awesome responsibility. I composed "The Bully" because, though years later, my heart still aches for that young man in that dismal algebra class.

Reflection Questions

1. For one day, take on the role of an outside observer in your school and record comments, behaviors, or actions that could be used as evidence that your school staff considers it a privilege to be around children. Share your list with colleagues. Is the list substantial or limited? What might your staff do to increase the atmosphere of teachers feeling privileged to be teachers?

   _____

   _____

   _____

   _____

   _____

   _____

2. The pressures of teaching are many. At a staff meeting, brainstorm ways teachers can support one another when frustration, fatigue, or disappointment is encumbering a teacher's attitude and effectiveness.

   _____

   _____

   _____

   _____

   _____

   _____

3. Most teachers would never engage in the behavior that was the basis for "The Bully." In a private reflection, examine whether there are subtle comments you or your colleagues may be making that can be hurtful to students. If the comments are yours, what can you do to remedy the situation? If the comments are your colleague's, what constructive action could you take to enlighten your colleague about the situation?

   _____

   _____

   _____

   _____

   _____

   _____

Extended Activity

Teachers cannot be at their best when they are drained of energy. Consider the following idea from Graves's *The Energy to Teach* (2001): "[M]aintain a one-week record of events in your life in school and at home. Rate these events or incidents for: *energy giving*, *energy taking*, and *a waste of time*" (p. 11). After one week, analyze your list. What conclusions can you make about what is feeding your spirit and what is draining it? Are there changes you can make that will increase the positive and, if possible, lessen the negative aspects of your experiences?

_____

_____

_____

_____

_____

_____

_____

_____

_____

_____

_____

_____

_____

_____

_____

_____

_____

_____

_____

_____

_____

_____

_____

_____

_____

A Man of Power

I met a man of power.

We talked upon a bench one Sunday afternoon.
I mentioned I was corporate manager
Of a prestigious operation;
But something in his manner made me feel
He had the power to control the world.

I casually informed him my income was six figures;
Yet I sensed he was richer than I.
Though I was puzzled by the wear of his shoes
And the simple design of an outdated watch
So I pursued.

I told him I was head of the campaign
To elect the city's highest official.
He told me he'd like doing that someday.
Immediately, I knew he was too busy shaping
Presidents or kings, or some future hero.

I shared with him my love of math
 (I was renowned for solving any problem).
He liked math, too,
But its mysteries seemed dwarfed when I felt
He daily dealt with issues of truth, and justice, and integrity.

No longer could I bear this average man,
Who, without his knowing,
Made my every gain seem second place.
So when parting, I introduced myself,
Aware my impressive title would surely right the situation.

He shook my hand and smiled.
And about to say his name,
He stopped instead to wave at a small child.
The child's beaming eyes reflected love and admiration,
And punctuated the greeting, "Hi, Daddy!"
They left—
One mighty hand clasped around a tiny palm.

I met a man of power.

Background: A Man of Power

Teachers indeed have tremendous influence over their students, but rarely more influence than the parents of those children. Thus, the importance of collaborating with parents about common goals and concerns cannot be overemphasized. Educators and researchers on school reform and culture consistently advocate for the inclusion of parents in the educational adventure of their children (Boyer, 1995; DuFour & Eaker, 1998; Harwayne, 1999). Current studies confirm that "parent engagement has a positive impact on students' academic achievement, behavior in school, and attitudes about school and work" (Boyer, 1995, p. 48). Schlechty (1992) reminds educators, "Most parents know their children much better than most teachers know them" (p. 46). For that reason alone, it behooves teachers to work with parents on ensuring the educational success of their students. However, there are some parents who will be reluctant to or will choose not to take part in their child's education. For example, one afternoon as I stopped in the school office to check my mailbox, I noticed that the school secretary looked dismayed. I asked what was troubling her, and she informed me that she had just called the father of a second-grade girl who was in the school clinic. The child had some kind of stomach flu and was quite upset. The secretary, unable to reach the child's mother, called the next number on the emergency card—the father's work number. When she finally got through to the father and explained his daughter's situation, he said, "Do you realize I had to put three people on hold to take this call?" I was shocked by the father's callous response to his little girl's plight. I wondered just to whom he was speaking that he felt those people were more important at that moment than his own child. My bewilderment about this incident led me to consider other times when this parent and other parents might not be available for their children's educational needs, and I transformed these thoughts into "A Man of Power."

Reflection Questions

1. Alice Keliher, educator in day-care policies and practices, stated, "If I could say just one thing to parents, it would be simply that a child needs someone who believes in him no matter what he does" (as cited in Clinton, 1996, p. 33). If *you* could say just one thing to parents, what would it be? Compare what you would say to what your colleagues might say.

_____

_____

_____

_____

_____

_____

2. Just as you would share an "if I could say only one thing" message with the parents of your students, invite them to share that same message with you. What do their responses tell you about their concerns and goals for their children?

_____

_____

_____

_____

_____

_____

3. What steps do you, as an individual teacher, and your school as a whole take to collaborate with parents, not just inform them, on the goals and concerns about their children's education? What evidence do you have that your efforts are successful? What additional measures do you take to reach parents who are absent or reluctant to engage in their children's schooling?

_____

_____

_____

_____

_____

_____

Extended Activity

Most teachers work hard independently to make parents feel welcome in their classrooms. As a staff, examine the message the school sends to parents about welcoming their presence. In *The Basic School: A Community for Learning* (Boyer, 1995), a report by The Carnegie Foundation for the Advancement of Teaching to explore significant issues in education, Boyer recommends that educators establish a "parent place"—"a comfortable location in the building where parents gather throughout the day and mingle, informally, with staff or other parents" (p. 58). If such a place is not feasible at your site, what other measures can be taken to especially recognize the importance and value of parental presence in your school?

The Lasting Gift

The teddy bear you gave to me
Was fun, and loved as it could be,
But meeting the Troll and the Wolf made me see
That fairy tales have lots of "three's";
And that "once upon a time" should mean
A "happily ever after" scene.

I loved the plastic dinosaur
And played with it for a year or more,
But in *Dinosaur Days* was the word *extinct*,
So when my teacher said, "Everyone think!"
I knew that I was able to give
The word that means species no longer live.

The poems I write and the songs I sing
Are rooted in all the rhymes you'd bring;
And the mysteries I now read with delight
Bring back our cuddling in bed at night
While reading *Encyclopedia Brown*—
The first books, I recall, I just couldn't put down.

Now that I've a tot of my own
I treasure the times when we're alone.
When we sit together and happily spend
Time reading old stories and meeting new friends;
And the most lasting gift you gave me is this—
Knowing "The end" comes with a hug and a kiss.

Background: The Lasting Gift

In the early 1990s, I taught in a relatively affluent neighborhood where most of my students' parents had college degrees. Therefore, I was shocked when I discovered that close to one fourth of my first-grade class had not been read to at home. During the Parent Night presentation held at the beginning of the school year, I highlighted the importance of reading aloud to children. One of the parents approached me afterward and frankly informed me that teaching his child to read was *my* job, not his. Obviously, I had not done a very effective job of convincing him (and perhaps the other parents) of the significance of reading aloud. I wondered if parents, as well as teachers, understood the contribution to educational success that reading aloud provides (Smith, 1988; Taberski, 2000; Trelease, 2001). Do they understand, as the first stanza of "The Lasting Gift" suggests, that children internalize story structure from hearing stories read aloud? Do they know that reading aloud is one of the most effective ways to increase interest in and knowledge of new vocabulary, as stanza two implies? Do they realize, as addressed in the third stanza, that the simple language play promoted by rhymes and riddles is a highly successful way to develop phonemic awareness, and that the love for a specific genre can develop early from reading "favorite stories"? Most important, are they aware of the social significance of language learning illustrated in stanza four? Smith (2003) discusses at length the importance of children gaining their identity as readers by wanting to belong to the "literacy club." That club is attractive to them because its members are people whom they love or admire or "want to be like." Yes, teachers can become those people, but for the most part it is parents who remain the most important and most influential people in a child's life. By reading with them, parents give their children an open invitation to join the "literacy club."

As I reflected on the year I taught kindergarten, I recalled the obvious difference in interest, vocabulary, and print concepts between the children who had been read to and the children whose experience with books was quite limited. I wrote "The Lasting Gift" to illustrate the great advantages one group of children will have over another simply by being in homes where they experience reading aloud.

Reflection Questions

1. Regardless of their grade level, there are benefits to reading aloud to students. If you do not already do so, plan a time—even just once a week—when you can share either a fiction or nonfiction selection with them. Brainstorm with a colleague about possible choices. What are your criteria for an appropriate read-aloud selection?

   _____

   _____

   _____

   _____

2. Echoing the thoughts of Regie Routman in her book *Conversations: Strategies for Teaching, Learning, and Evaluation* (2000), Ketch (2005) states, "All learning involves conversation. The ongoing dialogue, internal and external, that occurs as we read, write, listen, compose, observe, refine, interpret, and analyze is how we learn" (p. 9). Because of parents' and children's busy home lives, many parents not only have little time to read aloud to their children but also have limited occasions just to talk with them. Realizing that, outside of school, much knowledge is gained through conversation, examine some written assignments that your students are given for homework. Can any of those assignments be adapted to include conversation with a family member instead of written tasks? What are the benefits and limitations of such an assignment?

   _____

   _____

   _____

   _____

3. Spend some quiet time reflecting on your journey as a reader. Do you remember being read to? When do you first remember reading? What books, people, and experiences come to mind? Take some time to record your journey. You are a part of the journey your students are on. Where and in what light do you think they will fit you into their journey as readers?

   _____

   _____

   _____

   _____

Extended Activity

When teachers *and* parents model reading as a worthwhile and interesting activity, students receive two powerful invitations to join the "literacy club." Consider the advantages of having parents come into your classroom to read aloud to the students. Experiment with the idea and invite one or two parents to participate. Evaluate the impact the experience has on you, the parents, and your students. Is it worthwhile to continue? Why or why not?

Additional Resources About the Impact of Teachers and Parents

Allington, R. (1994). The schools we have. The schools we need. *The Reading Teacher, 48*, 14–29.

DeBruin-Parecki, A., & Krol-Sinclair, B. (Eds.). (2003). *Family literacy: From theory to practice*. Newark, DE: International Reading Association.

Skolnick, D. (2000). *More than meets the eye: How relationships enhance literacy learning*. Portsmouth, NH: Heinemann.

Trelease, J. (1993). *Read all about it! Great read-aloud stories, poems, and newspaper pieces for preteens and teens*. New York: Penguin.

Weissbourd, R. (2003). Moral teachers, moral students. *Educational Leadership, 60*(6), 6–11.

Section V

REFLECTIONS ABOUT

THE REWARDS
OF
TEACHING

"The single most important condition for literacy learning is the presence of mentors who are joyfully literate people."

SHIRLEY BRICE HEATH, PROFESSOR OF LINGUISTICS AND ENGLISH
AND LINGUISTIC ANTHROPOLOGIST

Memories of a First-Year Teacher

My first year as a teacher found me teaching a first grade.
I entered slowly that first day—excited and afraid.
My mind went blank: of college facts—remembered only traces,
My apprehension doubled greeting *48* first-grade faces!

    I didn't know the school routines;
    I didn't know the staff.
    I had to learn the playground schemes
    And the fire drill exit paths.
    I wasn't sure what books to use;
    What supplies there were at hand,
    Or that hanging artwork in the halls
    Would bring a reprimand.

But as enchanted days evolved my novice heart was lightened,
For children brought me smiles and hugs and made me feel less frightened.
Those dear ones taught me much that year (and every year thereafter),
But the firsts remain unique to me: their growth, their tears, their laughter.

    They were first to call me "Teacher."
    The first I taught to read.
    The first I thought about at night,
    Praying each one would succeed.
    Smiles graced with wiggly teeth,
    And freckled cheeks and noses;
    Squashed bouquets of dandelions
    More valuable than roses.

'Twas they who opened up my heart and filled it one by one;
Enriched it so I had the love to give to those who'd come.
They learned their facts and figures; favorite songs they sang;
And I learned that my heart would break when the final school bell rang.

    I'd miss their sweet behaviors
    And their simple, caring ways;
    I'd miss the stories read aloud
    And the questions they would raise.
    I'd miss the life that filled my room
    From my spirited 48.
    I had to give them up, I know,
    But it left a heart that ached.

When I recall my first attempts, apologies seem due.
Then I remember tenderness, and know this much is true:
Yes, there was much I had to learn, so much I didn't know!
But the enduring gift I gave to them was—oh, I loved them so.

Background: Memories of a First-Year Teacher

Believe it or not, I *did* have 48 first graders my first year of teaching. With everything else a new teacher has to learn, I had a crash course in how important it is to be organized. What a year! In spite of all the mistakes I made, and all the frustrations, it was a charmed year—the year that hooked me into teaching. I was thrilled to be a teacher and even then realized the importance of the message that Routman later conveyed in *Conversations: Strategies for Teaching, Learning, and Evaluating* (2000): "There is no other profession that excites and empowers me the way teaching does" (p. 1). Many years later, I attended an inservice workshop that began with a keynote speaker apologizing to her first class of students. The theme of the keynote address was how much more the speaker knows now because of experience and continual staff development. She stated that if she were to meet her first class of students now, all she could say would be "I'm sorry." Understanding exactly what she meant, and empathizing completely about how much I didn't know my first year, I still was troubled by that speech. I kept asking myself, "Would I apologize to my first class?" The more I thought about it, more of the details of that year came to mind. One detail that emerged was about one of my students who came from a dysfunctional family, one of those "heartaches in the classroom" Humphrey addresses in her poignant book *In the First Few Years: Reflections of a Beginning Teacher* (2003). This boy's parents were going through a heated custody battle. One afternoon, his mother met me after school and said she had to let me know what her son had said to the child advocate assigned to him: "Just tell them to give me to my teacher; she loves me." When I think of that, I know no matter what I didn't do for those children, I did love them. I cared about each and every one of them. And for that little boy, that made all the difference that year. I captured my reflections of that unforgettable year in "Memories of a First-Year Teacher."

Reflection Questions

1. Obviously, caring about our students is not enough to move them to the levels of knowledge and competencies expected from their schooling experience. Yet, the cliché "they won't care how much you know until they know how much you care" seems true for so many of us—students and teachers alike! Prioritize all you have to do in a given day. Is there time when you can build relationships with students? If so, how do you protect that time? If not, what might you be able to change to allow for such time?

   _____

   _____

   _____

   _____

2. For over 30 years, the results of the National Education Association (NEA) survey indicate that teachers' number one reason for entering the profession is their desire to work with young people (NEA, 2003). At the heart of the profession is the desire to make a difference in the life of a child. Think about the student to whom you have made the greatest difference. Why does that student come to mind? Write his or her name in a journal or on a piece of paper you can tuck away somewhere. Retrieve that journal or paper and look at the name on days when you become discouraged.

   _____

   _____

   _____

   _____

3. Change can indicate growth. Reflect on the most important change you have made since your first year(s) of teaching. Why do you consider that change to be so significant? Predict what change(s) may be in your future as a teacher. How do you see these changes contributing to the refinement of your teaching?

   _____

   _____

   _____

   _____

Extended Activity

Whether you are a novice teacher or a veteran teacher, write a brief reflection about your first year of teaching. What does that reflection reveal about your feelings of competency or anxiety? About feeling fulfilled or overwhelmed? Who or what made the year easier for you? What made it difficult? Use your reflection to help you, along with your colleagues, list ways you can support one another as teachers, especially teachers who are new to the profession.

My Teacher's Smile

I'm not a kid who actually likes school stuff.
It's hard to sit in desks and "keep it down."
There's only so much interest you can summon
About fractions, or who wore an English crown.

But in spite of all my struggles with this set-up;
I must confess I walk the extra mile.
Not for the grades, or for some added credit.
It's just because I love my teacher's smile.

She seems to know just when I've reached my limit,
And she catches me before I break the rule.
Then the smile she gives me whispers: "OK; calm down."
Hey, it's that smile of hers that's keeping me in school.

I bet she thinks it's all the words she tells me:
Like how smart I am; how she knows all I can do.
But she doesn't know how safe she makes me feel
When she smiles at me like I belong here, too.

Yeah, I don't like the "projects" or all that homework.
And for me, behaving sure can be a trial.
I won't get used to straight lines in the hallways,
But I'll work at it because it makes her smile.

I'll never be the poster kid for school days,
But I think I'll stick this out for just a while.
And I'll work, in spite of all my sound objections,
'Cause there isn't much that I won't do—to see my teacher smile.

Background: My Teacher's Smile

During my career in education, I had the opportunity to participate in a middle school and high school summer-school program. Although a few students were there to get a jump start on required courses, most of the student body had failed a required class during the previous school year and were hoping to get the necessary credit by passing the course in summer school. Needless to say, they were not happy to be there. Their tardiness, their apathetic behavior in the halls, and their general sense of frustration indicated that this was the last place they wanted to spend their summer. In my attempt to brighten the atmosphere, I made a point of standing at the entrance of the school each morning and greeting the students as they arrived, as well as wishing them a good afternoon at the end of the session. The last week of summer school, a young man approached me and asked me my name. He then said, "Well, you know, Mrs. Durica, you're the only teacher that smiled at me during this whole summer school thing." Not knowing anything about this particular student, unaware of just what part *he* may have played in this sad state of affairs, I was taken aback by his comment. I thought again about Harwayne's (1999) statement that she never hired a teacher unless she got the feeling that that person knew it was a "privilege to stand before students" (p. 5). I'm sure she did not mean just *successful* students. In *Education in a New Era*, Brandt (2000) states, "the real problem [with schools today] is that too many schools are without heart" (p. 113). Where were the joy, the enthusiasm, the encouragement, and the smiles of the privileged summer-school teachers? "My Teacher's Smile" was written in response to my asking, Where was the heart in this school?

Reflection Questions

1. When educator Frank Smith was asked how to teach a child who isn't interested in reading and writing, he responded, "You can't, won't, and shouldn't try" (Smith, 1983, p. 138). Expand that question and comment to learning in general. What do you think about that statement? Why do you think Smith responded that way? How do *you* teach children not interested in learning?

   _____

   _____

   _____

   _____

   _____

   _____

2. Students and teachers become frustrated by repeated failures. How or where do you find support when everything you have tried does not seem to be working? What do you do for students who feel the same way?

   _____

   _____

   _____

   _____

   _____

   _____

3. Ask your students to list the qualities of their favorite or best teacher. Examine the list for common trends. What does this information tell you about what your students value in their teachers? Do you also value those characteristics? Are any of those qualities present in your interactions with your students?

   _____

   _____

   _____

   _____

   _____

   _____

Extended Activity

Ask your colleagues to join you in this activity, which is an adaptation of an idea shared by Jeff Wilhelm at the 2006 CCIRA conference (Wilhelm, 2006). Each teacher individually lists all the people that possibly could be considered as having responsibility for a student's motivation to learn (e.g., the student, the parent, the teacher, the principal, last year's teacher, and so forth). Next to each person's name, record the percentage of responsibility you feel that person carries toward motivating the student. The sum of the percentages must equal 100. Compare your list with those of your colleagues. Where are there differences? How does this information influence your classroom instruction or practices?

_____

_____

_____

_____

_____

_____

_____

_____

_____

_____

_____

_____

_____

_____

_____

_____

_____

_____

_____

_____

_____

_____

_____

_____

Passion!

Who'd have thought that kids like us
Would get so into math?
We never liked those formulae
Or parabolic paths.
But the teacher assigned to algebra
Had fire in her eyes;
When she talked about equations,
We could see the fervor rise.
At first, she piqued our interest
By the way she carried on
About seeing mathematics
In our schoolwork and beyond.
She told tales of how math matters;
How it lives outside of school.
Then she called us math apprentices;
Made us think like scholars do.
She shared the lives of masters
Who made the field renowned,
And revealed how mathematics
Was truly *all* around.
And even though some tried to yawn
Each time we got our books,
Her love of solving problems
Finally got us hooked!
Her excitement was contagious;
We were captured by her zest.
And in spite of hesitation,
We began to do our best.
It's hard to be in company
Of lovers of an art
Without feeling you'd be losing out
If you chose not to take part.
Be it writing, learning language,
Searching facts still unexplored,
When you're in the midst of passion,
You just want to jump on board!
It seems the key to helping kids
To go beyond their reach
Is to care for them, and know your stuff,
And *love* what it is you teach!

Background: Passion!

I have a magnet on my refrigerator that shows a photograph of a toddler looking through a window at a baby bird that is looking right back at him. Below the picture is the following quote: "Show me a day when the world wasn't new" (The Borealis Press, www.borealispress.net/page3.html). What an exciting way to live a life, and what a meaningful mantra for educators, who spend their professional life revealing and reveling in ideas. The fact that as educators our worlds get to be "new" over and over again because of our students adds excitement as well as passion and joy to our work. I hope all of us can recall at least one teacher whose fire inspired us. And I hope we have the opportunity to display that fire to others.

The inspiration for this poem actually came from one of my adult students. I have had the great privilege and honor of being an adjunct instructor at the University of Colorado at Denver. The focus topic for one of the sessions of a literacy course I was teaching was spelling. I could tell by the disposition of the class as they entered that evening that they were not particularly looking forward to this session. Spelling—what a drag. Well, I have always found the history of English orthography fascinating. As our work continued, I could see more and more of the students becoming intrigued by what they had thought was just a discipline of straight memorization and rules. At the end of the session, one of the students came up to me and said, "You won me over. I guess I just never had a teacher who loved spelling before. I can't wait to try some of this with my students. This was one of the best classes I've ever had." I reflected on my own education and remembered teachers with passion who inspired me to learn in spite of my reservations. I recalled hearing educator Donald Murray say at the 1991 CCIRA conference that schools should be like zoos—with teachers in cages doing what they loved to do and students meandering through, selecting to go into a particular cage to learn a discipline from someone who was passionate about it (Murray, 1991). He felt students deserved that. All that came back to me with my student's comment about "winning her over" and gave rise to the poem "Passion!"

Reflection Questions

1. Realistically, it is not always possible to be passionate about what we teach. However, it is possible to build enthusiasm about what our students are learning. What steps do you take to remain interested in what you are teaching?

   _____

   _____

   _____

   _____

   _____

2. Human beings are innately motivated to learn. Learning is the natural state of the brain. Often, what drains life (and interest) from topics is spending time on incidentals rather than exploring the heart of the discipline. Think of a unit that, based on student response, seems particularly dry. What may be the cause? Are there elements about that topic that are significant, meaningful, and inherently appealing that are missed in the standard delivery of information and skill? Reflect on what truly makes that topic interesting. What changes can you make to excite your students about engaging in this unit? Keep in mind that the renowned scientist Albert Einstein once said, "I have no special talent, I am only passionately curious." What implication might that thought have to your unit?

   _____

   _____

   _____

   _____

   _____

3. Find out about the topics about which your students are passionate. Are there ways that those topics can be integrated with what needs to be studied?

   _____

   _____

   _____

   _____

   _____

Extended Activity

With a group of colleagues, share topics about which each of you is passionate—both academic and extracurricular topics. As a team, brainstorm possible ways some of that passion can be shared with students. For example, can you be guest lecturers in one another's classrooms? Can you establish a certain time each month or quarter when either you or your students pursue what you are passionate about? Be creative. Look for ways to breathe life and heart into your teaching.

_____

_____

_____

_____

_____

_____

_____

_____

_____

_____

_____

_____

_____

_____

_____

_____

_____

_____

_____

_____

_____

_____

_____

Who Has a Job That Is Better Than Mine?

I started the day with a kid named Fred,
Who told me that his cat was dead.
I began to express my sympathy
When he started to laugh and said with glee:
"Don't worry about it Mrs. D.
My cat's only *imaginary*!"

Now I know that the work can be a grind,
But who has a job that is better than mine?

Mid-morning the lesson began with long *e*.
We put words in sentences so we'd know
what they mean.
When I asked sweet Susannah,
our Georgia-born girl
To take the next word, and give "*heel*" a whirl,
She confidently said, with a voice so genteel:
"He got very tired when he walked up the heel."

Now I know that the pay is close to a crime,
But who has a job that is better than mine?

Playground duty was getting dull
When Carlos gave my sleeve a pull.
"That kid over there said the *e* word," he cried.
"Hon, I don't know such a word," I replied.
Startled, he looked up like I was a nut—
"Don't you know that he called me an *e*-diot!"

Now I know there are days you can lose
your mind,
But who has a job that is better than mine?

Afternoon brought our Thanksgiving Day play.
Teachers wore Native American costumes that day.
Erin took note of the blouse I'd chose,
Showing Pawnee dwellings in colored rows.
With pure innocence, she jabbed at my chest,
And said: "Mrs. D., I like your tepees best."

Now I know there are days when you work
9 to 9,
But who has a job that is better than mine?

Science class always ended our day.
Our dinosaur unit was underway.
Anne's report on mother dinosaur care
Caused David to suddenly gasp with despair.
"No!" he screamed, as he stomped the floor,
"You mean there were *GIRL* dinosaurs!"

Now I know there are days that you want to
resign,
But who has a job that is better than mine?

On my way home, I stopped for some gas;
Reached into my purse to get out some cash,
When a paper all gummy with raspberry jam
Came out with the dollars and stuck to my hand.
Peeling it off, I read through the goo:
"Surpriz, Mrs. D.! I reely luv you."

Now let me ask you one last time,
Who has a job that is better than mine?

Background: Who Has a Job That Is Better Than Mine?

Throughout my career in education, I always had so many stories to share about my students. My colleagues would make a comment like "Well, Karen, what did they do today?" One year, one of my grade-level colleagues seriously said, "Karen, you're so lucky. You always get the funny students." Well, it didn't take much reflection to know that I didn't get students any funnier than she did; I just realized how funny they were. I appreciated the lightness they brought to the classroom atmosphere with their perceptions of the world and their genuine spirits. I relished their zest for and their excitement about the simplest events of life. From the naïveté of primary-grade children to the engaging humor of middle school and high school youth, the students offer us myriad opportunities for joy. We need to take advantage of these opportunities and not allow the business of our days to cloud them over.

As Graves (2001) reminds us in *The Energy to Teach*, we need to cultivate that which gives us strength and motivation in our work—that which feeds our spirit. I believe that the greatest source of energy for us is the students, if we take the time to appreciate them. This poem is based on actual events recorded in my journals; these charming and amusing incidents truly happened just as they are presented. The poetic license I took with this particular poem is that all the events did not occur on *one* day. What a delight to reread my journals and savor once again the joy my students have added to my life. "Who Has a Job That Is Better Than Mine?" highlights some of the examples of that joy. Composer Richard Wagner is credited with saying that "joy is not in things; it is in us." Indeed, it is in us, and it is in the remarkable students we teach.

Reflection Questions

1. Noonan (1990) states, "Humor is the shock absorber of life; it helps us take the blows" (p. 8). In what ways do you share your sense of humor with your students? Do they know what makes you laugh, and what doesn't? Do you know what different students in your class think is humorous, and what isn't? What role does humor play in your classroom milieu?

   _____

   _____

   _____

   _____

   _____

   _____

2. Critique your classroom for joy. Assume the role of an outside observer and, for one day, note moments of laughter, feelings of ease, or times when you and the students seem connected and comfortable. Analyze your notes. What does that information tell you about the relationships and atmosphere of your classroom?

   _____

   _____

   _____

   _____

   _____

   _____

3. What fuels your spirit? If it is something outside of your work, how can you connect that to your work and use that to help you maintain the joy of teaching? If it is your work itself that fuels your spirit, what steps can you take to maintain that positive flow?

   _____

   _____

   _____

   _____

   _____

   _____

Extended Activity

For one week, write down various statements or questions your students contribute, not just in formal classes but what you hear around you in the halls, at lunch, or on the athletic fields. What is joyful or humorous about what the students have said? What is poignant? Has noting their responses, reactions, and comments about life increased your appreciation of who they are? Consider opening grade-level or content-area meetings with different teachers sharing one example (names need not be given) of some joyful or poignant comment offered by a student. Speculate about what that practice may do to the tone of the meeting. Note: Be sure to take caution if a student comment, even if shared anonymously, would have been considered personal or private. Sharing stories about students must always be done with utmost respect for them.

_____

_____

_____

_____

_____

_____

_____

_____

_____

_____

_____

_____

_____

_____

_____

_____

_____

_____

_____

_____

_____

Additional Resources About the Rewards of Teaching

Barone, T. (2001). *Touching eternity: The enduring outcomes of schooling*. New York: Teachers College Press.

Fox, M. (1993). *Radical reflections: Passionate opinions on teaching, learning, and living*. San Diego, CA: Harcourt Trade.

Graves, D. (2002). *Testing is not teaching: What should count in education*. Portsmouth, NH: Heinemann.

Intrator, S., & Scribner, M. (Eds.). (2003). *Teaching with fire: Poetry that sustains the courage to teach*. San Francisco: Jossey-Bass.

Levine, S. (Ed.). (1999). *A passion for teaching*. Alexandria, VA: Association for Supervision and Curriculum Development.

References

Acton, J. (1948). *Essays on freedom and power*. Boston: Beacon.

Adler, M.J. (1984). *The paideia proposal: An educational manifesto*. New York: Macmillan.

Armon, J. (2003). Pathways to literacy: Addressing K–12 gender discrepancies in literacy achievement. *The Colorado Reading Council Journal, 14*, 31–37.

Barrs, M., & Pidgeon, S. (Eds.). (2003). *Boys and reading*. London: Centre for Language in Primary Education. Retrieved July 9, 2003, from http://www.staff.livjm.ac.uk/edcdwyse?Barrs%20Pidgeon.htm

Bauer, G. (2001). Why boys must be boys: Is your son's school giving him what he needs to succeed? *Canadian Living* [Electronic version]. Retrieved July 9, 2003, from http://www.readersdigest.ca/mag/2002/05/boys.html

Bear, D.R., Invernizzi, M., Templeton, S., & Johnston, F. (1996). *Words their way: Word study for phonics, vocabulary, and spelling instruction*. Englewood Cliffs, NJ: Prentice Hall.

Boyer, E.L. (1995). *The basic school: A community for learning*. Princeton, NJ: The Carnegie Foundation for the Advancement of Teaching.

Brandt, R.S. (Ed.). (2000). *Education in a new era*. Alexandria, VA: Association for Supervision and Curriculum Development.

Brooks, J.G., & Brooks, M.G. (1993). *In search of understanding: The case for constructivist classrooms*. Alexandria, VA: Association for Supervision and Curriculum Development.

Brophy, J.E. (1983). Research on the self-fulfilling prophecy and teacher expectations. *Journal of Educational Psychology, 75*(5), 631–661.

Brozo, W.G. (2002). *To be a boy, to be a reader: Engaging teen and preteen boys in active literacy*. Newark, DE: International Reading Association.

Cambourne, B. (1995). Toward an educationally relevant theory of literacy learning: Twenty years of inquiry. *The Reading Teacher, 49*, 182–190.

Canter, L., & Canter, M. (1994). *The high-performing teacher: Avoiding burnout and increasing your motivation*. Santa Monica, CA: Canter & Associates.

Clay, M.M. (1979). *The early detection of reading difficulties*. Portsmouth, NH: Heinemann.

Clinton, H.R. (1996). *It takes a village*. New York: Simon & Schuster.

Cooper, H.M., & Good, T.L. (1983). *Pygmalion grows up: Studies in the expectation communication process*. New York: Longman.

Cotton, K. (2006). Expectations and student outcomes. *School Improvement Research Series (SIRS)*. Retrieved February 25, 2006, from http://www.nwrel.org/scpd/sirs/4/cu7.html

Darling-Hammond, L. (1997). *Doing what matters most: Investing in quality teaching*. New York: National Commission on Teaching and America's Future.

DuFour, R., & Eaker, R. (1998). *Professional learning communities at work: Best practices for enhancing student achievement*. Bloomington, IN: National Educational Service.

Durica, K. (2004). An unleveled playing field: The ways in which school culture undermines and undervalues boys' writing. *The Colorado Reading Council Journal, 15*(1), 5-11.

Erwin, J.C. (2004). *The classroom of choice: Giving students what they need and getting what you want*. Alexandria, VA: Association for Supervision and Curriculum Development.

Ezarik, M. (2003). Study: Boys literate in spite of school. *District Administration, 39*(6), 58.

Field, R. (1971). Something told the wild geese. In M.H. Arbuthnot (Ed.), *The Arbuthnot anthology of children's literature* (3rd ed., p. 187). Glenview, IL: Scott Foresman.

Freppon, P.A. (2001). *What it takes to be a teacher: The role of personal and professional development*. Portsmouth, NH: Heinemann.

Gardner, H. (1983). *Frames of mind: The theory of multiple intelligences*. New York: Basic Books.

Gentry, J.R., & Gillet, J.W. (1993). *Teaching kids to spell*. Portsmouth, NH: Heinemann.

Glatthorn, A.A. (1994). *Developing a quality curriculum*. Alexandria, VA: Association for Supervision and Curriculum Development.

Goldberg, G., & Roswell, B. (2002). *Reading, writing, and gender: Instructional strategies and classroom activities that work for girls and boys*. Larchmont, NY: Eye on Education.

Goldberg, M.F. (2001). Balanced optimism: An interview with Linda Darling-Hammond. *Phi Delta Kappan, 82*(9), 687–690.

Good, T.L. (1987). Two decades of research on teacher expectations: Findings and future directions. *Journal of Teacher Education, 38*(4), 32–47.

Goodlad, J.I. (1984) *A place called school: Prospects for the future*. New York: McGraw-Hill.

Goodman, Y. (1985). Kid watching: Observing children in the classroom. In A. Jaggar & M.T. Smith-Burke (Eds.), *Observing the language learner* (pp. 9–18). Newark, DE: International Reading Association; Urbana, IL: National Council of Teachers of English.

Graves, D.H. (2001). *The energy to teach*. Portsmouth, NH: Heinemann.

Guzzetti, B.J., Young, J.P., Gritsavage, M.M., Fyfe, L.M., & Hardenbrook, M. (2002). *Reading, writing, and talking gender in literacy learning*. Newark, DE: International Reading Association; Chicago: National Reading Conference.

Harwayne, S. (1999). *Going public: Priorities & practice at The Manhattan New School*. Portsmouth, NH: Heinemann.

Heubert, J.P., & Hauser, R.M. (Eds.). (1999). *High stakes: Testing for tracking, promotion, and graduation*. Washington, DC: National Academy Press.

Humphrey, T. (2003). *In the first few years: Reflections of a beginning teacher*. Newark, DE: International Reading Association.

International Reading Association. (1999). *High-stakes assessments in reading* (Position statement). Newark, DE: International Reading Association.

Jaeger, R.M., & Hattie, J.A. (1995). Detracking America's schools: Should we really care? *Phi Delta Kappan, 77*(3), 218–219.

Ketch, A. (2005). Conversation: The comprehension connection. *The Reading Teacher, 59*, 8–13.

Kohn, A. (1993). *Punished by rewards: The trouble with gold stars, incentive plans, A's, praise, and other bribes*. New York: Houghton Mifflin.

Lipton, L., & Wellman, B. (with Humbard, C.). (2003). *Mentoring matters: A practical guide to learning-focused relationships* (2nd ed.). Sherman, CT: MiraVia.

Longfellow, H.W. (1971). Paul Revere's Ride. In M.H. Arbuthnot (Ed.), *The Arbuthnot anthology of children's literature* (3rd ed., p. 40). Glenview, IL: Scott Foresman.

Lyons, C.A., & Pinnell, G.S. (2001). *Systems for change in literacy education: A guide to professional development*. Portsmouth, NH: Heinemann.

Millard, E. (1997). *Differently literate: Boys, girls, and the schooling of literacy*. London: Falmer.

Mulac, A., & Lundell, T.L. (1982). An empirical test of the gender linked language effect in a public speaking setting. *Language and Speech, 25*(3), 243-256.

Murray, D. (1991, February). Reading the blank page: How writers read the unseen text. Keynote address presented at the Colorado Council, International Reading Association conference, Denver, CO.

National Association for the Education of Young Children. (1997). *Developmentally appropriate practice in early childhood programs serving children from birth through 8*. Washington, DC: Author.

National Education Association. (2003). *Status of the American public school teacher 2000-2001: Highlights* [Electronic version]. Washington, DC: Author. Retrieved February 25, 2006, from http://www.nea.org/edstats/images/statushighlights.pdf

Newkirk, T. (2002). *Misreading masculinity: Boys, literacy, and popular culture.* Portsmouth, NH: Heinemann.

Noonan, P. (1990). *What I saw at the revolution: A political life in the Reagan era.* New York: Random House.

Peterson, S. (2002). Gender meanings in grade eight students: Talk about classroom writing. *Gender and Education, 14*(4), 351–366.

Routman, R. (2000). *Conversations: Strategies for teaching, learning, and evaluating.* Portsmouth, NH: Heinemann.

Routman, R. (2002). Teacher talk. *Educational Leadership, 59*(6), 32–35.

Sadker, D. (2002). An educator's primer on the gender war. *Phi Delta Kappan, 84*(3), 235–240, 244.

Schlechty, P.C. (1992). *Creating schools for the 21st century.* San Francisco, CA: Jossey-Bass.

Schlechty, P.C. (1997). *Inventing better schools: An action plan for educational reform.* San Francisco: Jossey-Bass.

Schlechty, P.C. (2002). *Working on the work: An action plan for teachers, principals, and superintendents.* San Francisco, CA: Jossey-Bass.

Smith, F. (1983). *Essays into literacy: Selected papers and some afterthoughts.* Portsmouth, NH: Heinemann.

Smith, F. (1986). *Insult to intelligence: The bureaucratic invasion of our classrooms.* Portsmouth, NH: Heinemann.

Smith, F. (1988). *Joining the literacy club: Further essays into education.* Portsmouth, NH: Heinemann.

Smith, F. (1994). *Writing and the writer* (2nd ed.). Hillsdale, NJ: Erlbaum.

Smith, F. (2003). *Unspeakable acts, unnatural practices: Flaws and fallacies in "scientific" reading instruction.* Portsmouth, NH: Heinemann.

Smith, M.W., & Wilhelm, J.D. (2002). *"Reading don't fix no Chevys:" Literacy in the lives of young men.* Portsmouth, NH: Heinemann.

Snow, C.E., Burns, M.S., & Griffin, P. (Eds.). (1998). *Preventing reading difficulties in young children.* Washington, DC: National Academy Press.

Stewart, D., Prebble, T., & Duncan, P. (1997). *The reflective principal: Leading the school development process.* Katonah, NY: Richard C. Owen.

Stiggins, R. (1996). *Student-centered classroom assessment.* Englewood Cliffs, NJ: Merrill.

Taberski, S. (2000). *On solid ground: Strategies for teaching reading, K–3.* Portsmouth, NH: Heinemann.

Tomlinson, C. (1999). *The differentiated classroom: Responding to the needs of all learners.* Alexandria, VA: Association for Supervision and Curriculum Development.

Trelease, J. (2001). *The read-aloud handbook* (5th ed.). New York: Penguin.

Wilhelm, J.D. (2006, February). Inquiring minds learn to read and write: Promoting engagement and achievement through questioning and discussion strategies. Presentation at the Colorado Council, International Reading Association conference, Denver, CO.

Winebrenner, S. (1996). *Teaching kids with learning difficulties in the regular classroom.* Minneapolis, MN: Free Spirit.

Wolfe, P. (2001). *Brain matters: Translating research into classroom practice.* Alexandria, VA: Association for Supervision and Curriculum Development.

York-Barr, J., Sommers, W., Ghere, G., & Montie, J. (2001). *Reflective practice to improve schools: An action guide for educators.* Thousand Oaks, CA: Corwin Press.

Photographs

Image accompanying "How We 'Do' School" © 2006 Jupiter Images Corporation

Image accompanying "I Used to Ask the Questions: Kindergartner's Lament" © 2005 Comstock Images

Image accompanying "Museums of Their Souls" © 1999 Comstock Images

Image accompanying "The Feel of a Pencil" © 1999 Comstock Images

Image accompanying "When Spelling Rules" © 2006 Jupiter Images Corporation

Image accompanying "Chapter 14" © 2006 Jupiter Images Corporation

Image accompanying "Dearth of Dictionary Learning" © 2006 Jupiter Images Corporation

Image accompanying "I Read It Because It's Beautiful" © 2005 Comstock Images

Image accompanying "The Labeled Child" © 1999 Artville

Image accompanying "My Friend's G/T" © 2006 Jupiter Images Corporation

Image accompanying "I'm Partially Proficient" © 2001 PhotoDisc

Image accompanying "Unloved Stories: A Poem for Two Voices" © 2001 PhotoDisc

Image accompanying "The Man Who Let Me Speak" © 2005 Comstock Images

Image accompanying "The Bully" © 2002–2005 Veer Incorporated

Image accompanying "A Man of Power" © 2002 Photo Alto

Image accompanying "The Lasting Gift" © 2006 Jupiter Images Corporation

Image accompanying "Memories of a First-Year Teacher" © 1999 Comstock Images

Image accompanying "My Teacher's Smile" © 1999 Comstock Images

Image accompanying "Passion!" © 2006 Image Source

Image accompanying "Who Has a Job That Is Better Than Mine?" © 2005 Comstock Images

Index